THE EXILE
was originally published by
The John Day Company, Inc.
in association with Reynal & Hitchcock.

Pearl S. Buck

The Exile

PUBLISHED BY POCKET BOOKS NEW YORK

THE EXILE

John Day edition published 1936

POCKET BOOK edition published February, 1964

3rd printing .... January, 1976

L.

This POCKET BOOK edition includes every word contained
in the original, higher-priced edition. It is printed from
brand-new plates made from completely reset, clear, easy-to-
read type. POCKET BOOK editions are published by POCKET
BOOKS, a division of Simon & Schuster, Inc., 630 Fifth
Avenue, New York, N.Y. 10020. Trademarks registered
in the United States and other countries.

The
Exile

I

OUT of the swift scores of pictures of her that pass through my memory I choose one that is most herself. I take this one. Here she stands in the American garden she has made in the dark heart of a Chinese city on the Yangtse River. She is in the bloom of her maturity, a strong, very straight figure, of a beautiful free carriage, standing in the full, hot sunshine of summer. She is not tall, nor very short, and she stands sturdily upon her feet. There is a trowel in her hand; she has been digging in her garden. It is a good, strong hand that holds the trowel, a firm brown hand not too whitely well kept, and bearing evidence of many kinds of labor. But it is shapely in spite of this, and the fingers are unexpectedly pointed and delicate at the tips.

The tropical sun beats down on her but she holds her head up to it, unafraid, and her eyes are open and clear to it, hazel brown eyes, gold-flecked, under dark brows, very direct in their gaze and set in short, thick, black lashes. At this time in her life one did not stop to see

7

whether she was beautiful or not. One was caught and held with the vigor and the strength of life in her face, a straight nose not too small and with a good wide space between the eyes, a mobile mouth, very expressive and changeful, its lips not too thinly cut, a small, firm, well-shaped chin and beautiful neck and shoulders. The sun falls hotly upon her hair. It is thick and soft and curls about her face. In color it is a warm chestnut, except where she has swept it up from her temples and there, above her low, broad forehead, it shows two wings of white, and where it is heaped upon her head in a great full knot, the white mingles again and again in the strands.

Strange strong figure there in that American garden she has made in the dark heart of a Chinese city! She could pass for none other than an American, although the foreign sun has burned her skin browner than is its nature. A lounging Chinese gardener leans against a bamboo that is one of a cluster near her, his blue cotton coat and trousers girdled loosely at his waist, a wide hat made of bamboo splits upon his shaven crown.

But neither bamboo nor gardener can make her exotic. She is quite herself. Indeed, he has had little to do with that garden of hers, beyond carrying buckets of water for its watering. It is she who has planted American flowers there, wallflowers and bachelor's buttons and hollyhocks against the enclosing brick wall of the compound. It is she who has coaxed the grass to grow smooth and clipped under the trees and has set a bed of English violets against the foot of the veranda. Over the ugly, angular lines of the mission house she has persuaded a Virginia creeper to climb, and it has covered two sides already. At one end of the long veranda a white rose hangs heavy with bloom, and if you go near it she will call you sharply away, for there is a turtle dove's nest there and she is guarding it as zealously as the mother bird guards it. Once I saw her angry—and she can be angry often—because that lounging gardener robbed the nest, and she poured out on him a torrent of well-articulated Chinese, and he skulked astonished from her presence. Then in a passionate pity she turned to the fluttering mother bird and her voice fell until one would not have said it was the same voice, and she coaxed the mother bird and twisted the rose branches this way and that and picked up the despoiled nest and put it tenderly back, and sorrowfully and angrily she gathered the broken eggshells together and buried them. And who more joyous than she when the mother bird laid four more small eggs in the replaced nest!

"Now that was good and brave of her!" the woman cried, her eyes flashing.

But this picture of her in the American garden she made in a strange country is not the beginning. It does not explain her, nor how, forever American as she was, she came to be making the garden in China, if, indeed, she can ever be explained. Nevertheless, the beginning at least must be told.

Her family sprang from sturdy, well-to-do, independent Dutch stock. Her grandfather had been a thriving merchant in the city of Utrecht in Holland. In that day of hand labor he was accounted rich, for he owned a factory that employed a hundred artisans, and there he made cabinet furniture from imported woods. Out of that factory, doubtless, came many of the desks of rosewood and the inlaid tables and mahogany pieces of that time.

This Dutchman, Mynheer Stulting, had a passion for fine workmanship and the perfection of detail. He was thrifty, too, and he laid up his money until it was considered that he had a fortune. He lived with his family in the typical city house of Utrecht, compact, comfortable, roomy, and full of solid, beautiful furniture, all of it neat and clean beyond imagination. He was essentially a city man, but he had his garden, a square garden at the back of the house, where he experimented, in a small way, with tulips and bulbs, and here he sat in the evening over his long pipe and his goblet of wine.

On the Sabbath day, which he held unalterably the Lord's day, he and his wife and their son, the youngest and the last at home, went to church. It would not have occurred to them to do otherwise, for among the three hundred souls who made up that church there was none to whom it was more important than to Mynheer Stulting, and he gave to it generously. He had a big voice and in church it rolled out of his short, thick throat, leading the psalms he loved to sing. His son, a slight, slender lad, stood beside him always, singing also. He was shorter than his father and much more slender in build, and meticulous in his garb. On the other side was his mother, large, soft, kindly, murmuring the tune of the psalm gently, her mind never quite detached from the immense Sunday dinner now warm in the porcelain oven of the stove in her spotless kitchen.

There was religion in that church of a Sunday morning. The pastor braced himself to it, a tall, lean whip of a figure, his eyes burning, his voice sonorous. To him there was at times a challenge well-nigh unbearable in the eyes of these three hundred souls who gathered without fail to hear him; fine, straight, level eyes, thinking, tranquil, hungering, critical. They knew well whether a man had been with God or not when he prepared his sermon. They expected solid meat, food for the brain, strength for the spirit. This he gave to them without sparing himself.

Then came the time, brief enough in history, of religious intolerance in Holland, and the burden of this intolerance fell upon these worshippers. On the Sunday following the issuance of the edict which took from them their freedom of worship, these three hundred met again, not this time to listen to their pastor, but to talk together of what they must do. As the quiet talk waxed fuller, it became evident that one thing at least was clear; these men and women would brook no interference with their religious liberty. It was Mynheer Stulting who at the end rose heavily to his feet and reared his thick neck back and flashed his dark, heavy-lidded eyes over the group. His great voice came forth like a trumpet call.

"As for me and my house," he cried, "we will serve the

10

Lord! If we cannot serve Him in our own country, then will we leave our country!"

He paused and gazed piercingly about him. Well they all knew there was not one of them who had more to lose than he, the goodly merchant! He paused and then he shouted sonorously,

"Let us go forth! Who will go?"

Quick as a dart of flame the white-haired pastor stood up, smiling in a sort of ecstasy. A score of young men sprang to their feet, their lips pressed together in straight lines, their eyes shining. Slowly the older men followed. They had more to lose: established businesses, thriving concerns, houses and lands. Last of all the women rose, a young woman here and there following with her eyes the leap of a lad to his feet and then, not too soon after, rising shyly. Last of all the mothers rose, holding little children pressed against them, their eyes troubled and frightened and greatly bewildered. At the end the three hundred souls stood, and their pastor, seeing them, felt the tears upon his cheeks for triumph that of such was his kingdom. He lifted his arms to pray and they fell upon their knees under the power of his look, and such prayer as went up filled the church with its force and presence. These were to go forth, forsaking all for the sake of God and liberty.

Of such stuff was this American woman made.

When the deep emotion of the day was over no whit of the determination passed. Mynheer with his solid Dutch thrift sold his factory at a good price and realized upon all he owned.

Nor would he make it too hard for his wife. She wept as she went about the house, but she wept softly and with her face turned away, for she would not do anything to move her husband away from his duty, nor did she indeed doubt that he knew far better than she what was God's will. She who was always busy at roasting and washing and cleaning and superintending the maidservants had little time to think of God and she must leave it to her husband. Besides, it took so long for her to spell out a few verses in the Book that she trusted to his reading the Scriptures morning and night, and it was a grief to her that even so in the morning her mind would of its own accord wander to the kaffee cake and to the sausage when she would fain have listened to the good word, and at night it was more shame still that do what she would she often fell asleep at prayer so that her husband had to awaken her and lift her from her knees. This made her humble, and the more humble because he never reproached her but only said in his big, kind way,

"Now, my good Huldah, how tired you are, aren't you?"

"Ach, Johann," she always replied contritely, "I want truly to hear the Good Word and why cannot I listen?"

Therefore if he said they must go she was sure they must, but he was not too hard upon her, and he let her take the things she loved most, and they packed huge boxes of feather beds and blue and white dishes and silver and what furniture they needed.

The two older sons were married and had their homes to break up, too, for they were all in the same church, but at Mynheer Stulting's house there was left Hermanus, the youngest son, who held himself so stiff and straight in his youth. He had not been put to the trade as the others had, for he was born late in his mother's life after the death of several children, and he was delicate. Moreover, when he grew to manhood there was enough and to spare in the prosperous house, and the lad was proud and sensitive and filled with the love of beauty, and his father and mother let him choose what he wanted to learn for a trade. He chose then to learn the craft of a jeweler, because he loved the color and touch of jewels, and he learned how to make and to repair watches, for he was fascinated with the instant and delicate precision of their fairy machinery.

Hermanus was on the whole a son surprising from these stocky, thrifty parents. Standing between them in the church pew, or mingling with his sturdy brothers and their wives and children, he seemed alien from them in some way, small and slight and dreaming as he was, great only in his pride and independence, so that not one of them thwarted him if it could be helped. Moreover, he was better educated than the others, for he had demanded to be taught many things. He spoke several languages and he wrote music and verse and he was clever with his pencil and with pen and ink and drew exquisitely. He had besides these gifts a beautiful singing voice and an ear trembling and keen for true pitch. Early in his life others had recognized this gift, and when he was scarcely more than a boy he held the tuning fork in the church and set the tune for the psalms.

Of the stuff of this lad, delicate, flaming, proud, loving beauty to passion, was this American woman made also, for he was her father.

Sometimes the younger son was sent on journeys to other places for Mynheer Stulting, and this he loved. He would flaunt himself a little when he was away, and he bought a gay waistcoat in Amsterdam, or a high silk stock, and he delighted to wear his linen spotless and was fastidious in his perfumes and in the cut of his coat. Nevertheless, he could always be trusted, even had he not taken with him a faithful servant, for that very fastidiousness kept him from the crude sins of young men, that and his intense pride in himself.

When Mynheer was finishing the business of his house preparatory to leaving his country there were certain houses that owed him money, for the retail shops of many cities were glad to buy the perfected pieces of furniture he made, each piece scrutinized by him and many polished finally by his own hands. So he sent his son and he said, "Hermanus, go to Amsterdam one more time and this time see yourself the head of this house and clear up all accounts. Tell him I leave my country that I may be free and it is the end and the beginning."

The owner of this house to which Mynheer sent his son was a Frenchman of Huguenot blood, who had inherited monies from his father, and Hermanus had been to see him before and there he had met the young daughter. Each time he had been more deeply fascinated by the tiny dark-eyed maid, lighter and more fragile than the fair Dutch girls he knew, and short as he was, she was scarcely above his shoulder. Nevertheless, so strict were the customs of the country that they had never talked together alone, although the last three times they had met they had looked at each other and their eyes had melted together and he knew that one day more must be said between them.

Now he knew he was seeing her for the last time, She sat with her little, dark, curly head bent over her embroidery frame, demure and silent, as he delivered his father's message, and when she heard that he was to go to a foreign country, she looked up, panting a little, and he saw her put her hand upon her breast. Suddenly and in that instant the fluttering warm excitement in his own breast that he had scarcely called love grew and spread and well-nigh choked him and he knew he must have this small French maid. Then stammering and flushed and aching with pride and fear he asked the father's permission to pay his addresses to the daughter. The old man instantly sent his daughter from the room and his black eyebrows darted over his forehead, his eyes opening and shutting and his shoulders shrugging and fingers waving, and he was astonished at what had happened. Nevertheless, he would not say yes or no, for he knew the young man's father was wealthy, and so he temporized and spoke of an arrangement later.

"But I am going far from my country," said Hermanus steadily, suddenly bold. "It must be at once."

Ah, then, it was impossible, the darting eyebrows and fluttering eyelids proclaimed, and Hermanus turned haughtily away, his heart beating wildly under his still breast and proud face.

When he reached the street he could have wept for all his pride, and he stumbled along the cobbled street to his hotel, blind because he could not see for his tears. He could not delay his departure beyond that night, since the business was finished. Then, incredibly, he heard soft steps running behind him, and there behind him she was, her hair muffled in a little lace shawl, and she seized his arm and poured out words upon him. Was he going away? Ah—to America? Ah—so far as that? Ah—it was very far! And her eyes dropped suddenly, pretty, frank, child-like eyes, brown, flecked with gold. Hermanus looked at her in despair. Somehow into this moment must be crowded months of slow and courteous courtship. His Dutch directness came to his aid. He said plainly, "Will you have me for your husband?"

She looked up at him then, swiftly and frankly. "Yes, I will," she said.

Then they planned quickly. She was alone in the house except for her old father and the housekeeper—her mother was long dead—yes, she could escape easily enough. Yes, she could meet him in half an hour and they could take the carriage then. Yes, she was quite sure —it was not new to her—she had told herself that if he asked for her she would have him. She would go to his parents—to America.

Hermanus stood waiting for her in that quiet, twisted street, in a fever of love and fear, not unmixed with embarrassment, and sooner than she had said she came running to him again in her little bonnet and cloak. He took her to his hotel where his manservant awaited him, and in spite of that phlegmatic man's horror, the two coaxed and had their way and the next morning presented themselves before Mynheer Stulting and his wife, pale and exhausted with the night's travel, but determined and indomitable.

This power for passion and love went also into the making of the American woman, for these were her parents.

The congregation could not leave Utrecht as quickly as they had planned. Three hundred people cannot so quickly tear up their roots. Besides, there were those who hoped for a change in the policy of the government. But the change did not come and so within the year all preparations were made. This year gave time after the marriage of Hermanus to his little French maid, and gave time also for the birth of Hermanus's son, whom they named Cornelius, and so when the hour came for departure, there were three generations of the Stulting family to sail away from their country.

Three hundred souls, then, with their pastor at their head, sailed across the Atlantic Ocean. They chartered a ship to carry them all together, and upon it they lived quietly, facing the unknown future steadily, making practical plans of what they would do. It took them nearly twenty days to cross the ocean and eight of their number died of influenza. These they buried at sea, and the pastor prayed as they lowered the bodies into the waves, his thin white hair tossed by the sharp sea winds.

But to Hermanus and his wife it was a time of love and exaltation. It meant little to them that the old French father had sent word that although he forgave his daughter he did not wish her to come home again.

"How could I go home, anyway?" she cried gaily when she heard of it. "Besides, I have never loved him. He is a cruel old man. Ah, 'Ermanus!"

Hermanus was enchanted the more because she could never pronounce his name except with the soft French elision of its consonants. Where they were going he scarcely knew. He trusted to his father in this as in everything. Meanwhile here was his love beside him, and here their little son.

Once upon the American shores their difficulties began. They were not a sentimental people and they thought more now about practical questions of how to live than they did of the impulse that had moved them to liberty. It was well, for the people in New York were greedy and clever and when the shipload of thrifty Dutch merchants and artisans sailed into harbor they were fair prey and these prosperous-looking Dutchmen had to hand out gold pieces for the slightest necessary service.

But they bore this with fortitude and proceeded at once to land in Pennsylvania they had bought on paper. When they reached there this land proved to be entirely swamp and fitted for nothing and there was no hope of farming it. It had been the wish of all to settle together in one spot where they could establish homes and business and church in a unit. There were those who were discouraged and turned back to the towns, to which they were more used. Mynheer Stulting was not one of these. He stood up on the wet, boggy land as he had stood in the church, and he called to those who would follow him and their pastor and they would buy more land to the south with what was left of their gold and thus stay together. Out of the less than three hundred, more than a hundred stood up silently to follow him. Land was then bought in Virginia and they went there, grimly and in sorrow of heart and homesickness. But the land this time was good, a high, level, fertile plain set among encircling mountains. Yet how strange and hard it was to these city-bred men and women, accustomed to the busy ease of living in the wealthy Dutch city, and knowing nothing of farming and country life even in their own small, compact, well-cultivated country! Here there were wild mountains all about them and upon the land where they must live stood great forests. A little English settlement was near, but the Indians marched around them and through their land, and these, while fortunately not actively hostile, were frightening and savage to see.

Nevertheless, the Dutch were stout-hearted, and they bartered what they could for hatchets and axes and knives, and they hacked down trees, following such instructions as were given them by the English. Each family built a crude cabin of logs for itself and then they joined together and built a larger one for a church. On the first Sunday in this church, where the pews were felled logs with the bark still on, and the pulpit a great stump, these people met together under an alien sky, which now they must make their own, to worship the God for whom they had left so much. Many of their number moved on again in those first two years, for the difficulties and deprivations of the life had been too much for the older ones and the more delicate of the city-bred folk, and of those who stood up to praise God there were only between fifty and sixty, and many of these, though they praised, had tears running down their cheeks. But their pastor was still there, a figure wraith-like and pitiably aged, but indomitable still. Within the next year he also died.

What work had to be done in those first years! They had to clear fields and plant crops to feed themselves. The trees were chopped down first and hauled away with chains pulled by horses and men together, and the stumps were left standing until the more pressing work of seed planting and harvesting was finished. Then during the winters the great stumps were dug about and chains attached again and with deep groaning and heaving men and horses wrenched them from the earth. Set on one side these stumps made the first fences the people had. But it was agonizing labor. Soon one would never have known there was a city-bred man among them except for Hermanus. His slight figure was too slender to be of much value where brawn was needed, and he maintained in spite of everything his fastidious, slightly dandified air. Even here in the wilderness he tinkered at his craft, and people who had watches and clocks brought them to him sometimes from long distances.

Hermanus and his wife and children lived in a log cabin adjoining that of his parents. The intrepid little French woman from Paris had made a marvelous pioneer. Gay in spite of every hardship, fleet of foot and swift of hand, practical and passionate, she flew at her tasks, keeping the cabin immaculate, caring for the babies as they came year by year, three little girls after Cornelius, and then a son. Then she rested from children for a few years.

This small woman never ceased to adore her husband.

To her he was fine, too fine for this life. As for herself, she could accept it. One had to cook, to sew, to care for one's children; everywhere women had such things to do, and she could do them here also. She dug industriously at a patch of garden, she walked ten miles to the settlement and brought back a setting hen and six fresh eggs and began a flock. She bemoaned the fact that there was a pool but no duck eggs—in France ducks were so nice! Every day she washed a shirt for her husband and ironed it, a shirt of white cloth that she had made herself. He did not rise in the morning before eight and she took him a cup of chocolate always before he breakfasted. It did not occur to her that before he came to the table for his coffee and cakes she had already done half a day's work for the family. She adored him and delighted in his gentlemanly ways and in his fresh looks and shaven cheeks and in his immaculate white shirt and collar. There was not another man in the settlement like him.

Perhaps more quickly than any of the more stolid Dutch women this little French woman learned to adapt herself to the wilderness and to turn its waste into a garden, a neat French garden. Here and there she gathered slips and twigs. It seemed as though she could never go to anyone's home without coming back with a root of something tied tenderly in her kerchief. Her family throve on her vegetables and chickens and eggs and she coaxed a calf from an English neighbor in exchange for sewing done, and they had milk to drink and were among the first to have it.

She was so practical and so gay that one would have said she made nothing of the wilderness and the labor she had to do in it. But one day she came home from her potato patch and at the door of the cabin she paused a moment to look and see if her baby were safe as she lay sleeping in the little wooden crib made from a hollowed log. The baby was asleep, but to the mother's horror, a rattlesnake lay across the child, stretched and at ease, coiling and uncoiling its length slowly!

The mother leaned faint against the lintel. Her swift

19

brain told her not to make a sound or movement. But what if the child should wake or move? She sank silently upon the doorstep and watched, weak with fright, and prayed desperately. There she sat, and the snake lay at ease and uncoiled. The sun rose higher and soon it would be time for the others to come home for the noon meal. She prayed on. At last, indifferently, the snake began to move, and dragging itself along it slipped over the edge of the crib and upon the earthen floor and moved toward the crack between two logs.

Then anger filled this small, valiant mother. She seized the hoe she had in her grasp and she flew at the surprised snake, striking and beating and screaming at it. When Hermanus came in there she lay stretched on the ground, fainting and weeping beside the mangled snake, and the child had awakened and was playing peacefully. It was the first time he had ever seen her weep.

The next child to be born was Carie, and into the making of this child went the best of her mother's maturity, the gayety, the common sense, the courage and the adaptability, the passion and the temper of this small French mother.

The life of the Dutch settlement now began to be built into the life of the American nation. This these people did consciously and of their own will, although there were among the older ones some who longed, as did even Mynheer Stulting at times, for the comfort and security of his old home. It had been a sad blow to him when the pastor died in the early years and he was never again satisfied altogether with any who tried to take his place.

Hardest of all to bear was the word that within six months after they had left home the government reversed its policy and gave liberty of worship to its citizens. If they had only been patient a little longer all this need not have been, all this bitter labor, these dead! There were those who blamed Mynheer Stulting now for being too impetuous. He looked at them with pleading, humbled eyes, stunned for what he had done. He whispered from a dry throat, "But still it was for God and liberty!"

Then his good wife came to his aid and she stood before his accusers and said in her soft voice, the first and only time one had ever heard her speak in the congregation, "How then could we have foreseen it? The good God knows now at least that we were willing to leave all and follow Him. Now He knows us for what we are. We have proved ourselves. And who of you gave up more than my man, and what woman more than I, who had a good house with twelve rooms and a porcelain stove in every room?"

It was true, and no more was said, until Mynheer at last said resolutely, "To go back is impossible. We can only go forward. We must build ourselves into this new nation. Let our children be taught to use the language of this country, and we ourselves so far as we are able to learn it. Let us obey its laws and become its citizens, and be no more the citizens of the old country."

And thus they set themselve to do thereafter.

It was the dream of Mynheer that before he died he would one day have a house like the one he had in Holland, and he thought if he had it he would forget more easily his memories. This he felt the more because he saw his wife yearned for a house, a real house, and that she never felt at home in the rude log rooms.

The land they had was rich and the older sons of Mynheer farmed it well and for some years there was besides food some money left at the end of the year. There was plenty of wood, and a small sawmill in the English settlement, and so Mynheer decided to build the house he wanted. He planned it and worked on it eagerly himself, and the sons put in their spare time on it, and it delighted him to see his good old wife, who had borne all so patiently in spite of her bewilderment, rejoicing in the house.

There at the edge of the settlement they built it, a goodly, twelve-room house of wood, with smooth floors and plastered and papered walls, a city house. The wood they took from their own lands and such of the labor as they could not supply themselves they exchanged. But it took a long time to build, more than two years, and before the house was finished the second winter fell, the intense, bitter winter of the mountains, and Mynheer took a chill as he stood and watched the house being built, and before they knew he was ill scarcely, he was ill to death and was gone. In the same winter his wife, caring nothing now for the house, faded softly and gently out of life.

These two, passing out of the new country, to one yet more new to them, looked on their granddaughter, Carie, in her cradle, although of this she had no memory. But in her brain and in all her flesh she bore their imprint.

A wave of discouragement passed over the settlement that winter of 1858. Crops had not been good, and several of the Dutch men decided to give up farming and go to some town, into business. The two older sons of Mynheer were among these and they took their families and went away. Then there were left only Hermanus and his family and the unfinished house.

But the little boy who had been born in the old country was now nearly fifteen years old, and wise and responsible for his years, and with his help Hermanus finished the house with such other labor as he could get, and they moved into it. Carie at this time was two years old, and her earliest memories were of this new house and of its big, square, empty rooms.

This home, then, spacious, dignified, beautiful, fashioned out of the mind of Mynheer, her grandfather, and finished by the eager young hands of her brother, went into the making of this American woman.

At this point Carie can begin to tell her own story as she remembered it, and as she told it to me through many years after she had gone to China. There was never any time when she spent long hours at the telling. She was ever too busy a woman to spend hours at talk. But looking back over the thirty years in which I knew her, I find, piecing this to that, a very clear picture before me of her youth and girlhood in what grew during those earlier years to be a small town in Virginia, built on the high fertile plain in the mountains called Little Levels.

Usually on Sunday evenings she would tell me more than at any other time. There was something about Sunday to her that made keen her memories of home. On Sunday mornings she rose with a look different from that of other days upon her face. There was less of purpose and planning and more of peace. Her low, square brow was smooth and her bright eyes, usually more sparkling than serene, were tranquil.

Breakfast in the sunny dining room of the mission house on Sunday was always cheerful. I remember it in a mingling of shining white cloth, always a pot of flowers on the table with the latest opened flowers in it, fruit, hot coffee, southern hot bread, preserves, bacon and eggs. A yellow Chinese boy darted about the table to serve, and she directed him a little, her hands busy among the blue cups and saucers. Occasionally she looked lovingly out at her garden, always lovingly, whether it was in bloom, or whether it lay bare under winter skies.

"A pretty yard!" she would say.

Sometimes during the meal she would say, "A quiet Sabbath morning always makes me think of home. If I could only hear a church bell ringing! I remember how every Sunday morning at home my father marched to church with his Bible under his arm—straight as an arrow he was even at eighty!"

Church bells—she missed them always, their clear simplicity ringing out over quiet village homes. Occasionally through the day and often through the night there came floating up through the bamboos of the valley below the mission house the deep, somber sadness of the temple bell, beating its single, heartbreaking note. She hated it. To her it spoke of all the shadow and mystery and darkness of the Oriental life about her, and mystery and darkness she hated. When once a small Christian chapel in the city was dedicated she could not rest until she had sent back to her home village and persuaded people to

23

give money for a church bell, a little, cheerful church bell made in America, a lively bell that tinkled out its brisk tones along the Chinese streets, as American a greeting as one could imagine. I have often seen a stately old Chinese gentleman start as it began to peal out so gaily above him, and stop and crane his neck to stare at what it was. There was nothing so quick and clear in the whole city as that bell. Carie, hearing it on Sunday mornings, never failed to smile and cry out, "Now isn't that nice! It sounds like home."

But it was at the end of Sunday that she would talk most to us. Twice she had been to church; once in the morning to service in the Chinese chapel and again in the afternoon to that pathetic gathering of white men and women in a land far from home, who came desultorily together to worship the God of their remembrance. Both times she played the organ, achieving miracles of music out of microscopic baby organs. Every hymn she led, her beautiful, full soprano voice rising to the very rafters, a gay, lovely voice that remained big and clear even when her body later was shrunken to a wisp with illness.

Sunday evenings she sang, too, at her own organ. It was a gift to her from Cornelius who was her best beloved among her brothers and sisters, and who took a fathers' place with them because Hermanus remained all his life delicate and one whom they must foster rather than depend upon as a father. Did I say in the beginning that I remember her best in her American garden? I think I remember her as well in the little square living room of the mission house, a room she had made pretty and American with white curtains at the windows and fresh flowers and wicker chairs, sitting at her organ on Sunday evenings, singing. There with the dark tiled Chinese houses pressing against this American home, amid the shouts of vendors, the cries of children, the cursings and bawlings of the crowded street life, she sat and sang old hymns that transported us miles away across land and sea—"Nearer, My God, to Thee," "Abide with Me,"

"Jesus, Lover of My Soul." These and many more she sang, but she never failed to have in any group of hymns more of the triumphant ones; indeed the tones of her voice were by nature more fitted for mirth and for triumph than for sorrow and we liked best to hear her sing "I Know That My Redeemer Liveth" and "Rejoice, Ye Pure in Heart." Such were her favorites. At the end of her life when she lay dying she turned her head upon her pillow, her indomitable dark eyes shining in her little emaciated face, and she could say, "Don't sing anything doleful—sing the Glory Song over me!"

This clear voice of hers had always a quality of triumph in it, in spite of all the dark noisy life pressing about us. True, there were times when she could not sing at all, and at those times the whole house was heavy for us. But when she could sing again, and it was always soon, in that sweet room which had so little in it, I was transported back to the village in the Little Levels, and saw through her eyes the simple nobility of that early American life.

For when she had sung her heart contented and eased of its homesickness and quiet, and when we were held fast in the charm of her singing, she sat beside the fire with us if it were winter and if summer then out on the long veranda by the garden, and at such times, bit by bit as she thought to tell us, we saw her as child and maiden and young wife.

She made us see the big, beautiful house. There under its roof were her first memories. It was a big white house, three stories high, she said, and a gesture of her hand made us see it so. There was a deep, cool cellar underneath where they kept the shallow pans of milk and where they churned. There, too, on shelves were the round Dutch cheeses and casks of berry and grape wine. The berries they gathered in summer, blackberry and raspberry and elderberry. She broke off here sometimes to say reminiscently, "Every summer we used to go to the woods and gather those berries. I remember red raspberries with a sort of silvery dew on them. When wine was served I chose raspberry wine because it seemed to me it was still silvery and more sweet than the rest. My, how my bare legs were scratched by the briars!"

She stopped and smiled into the dusk and as she sat silent we saw the brown-legged little girl, deep in the berry patch, a sunbonnct over her head to protect her complexion.

"Not that it did any good," she always explained. "For I was brown as a nut myself, and terribly ashamed of it until Greta was born and she was even browner and so they stopped teasing me to tease her. Pretty she was, though, with her eyes big and black as a young foal's."

Later I was to see that house myself and it was just as she had said. There was a big yard in front fenced in with a wide gate in the fence, and one had to get down from the buggy or the surrey to unlatch it. There was an enormous old sugar maple to the left and there was a stile under it. Here many a time she led her horse to mount it, but that was when she was a young woman and her riding skirt was long and tripped her when she walked. When she was a little girl she ran into the meadow and caught a horse by its mane and leaped on its back as it ran, her curly dark hair streaming.

"That lovely freedom," she used to muse. "I just ache for these little Chinese girls when I remember myself running and leaping on a horse and dashing over the little hills and valleys. And to think that they have only these old muddy water buffaloes, idling along the roads!" Her eyes, swift to speak, looked out troubled over the huddled Chinese roofs beyond the garden wall.

Around the white house that had been her childhood home there were wide spaces, and about the doorway a flower garden and flagged path leading to the square porch that had vines covering its open sides, and wooden seats in the green shadows. A big white door faced one, then, thrown wide in all seasons but winter, and there was a brass knocker on it and above it a fan-shaped glass window. When I was there the door stood open and I looked straight into a broad long hall and out the other end onto a lawn and trees and phlox beds against a fence and beyond that into the apple orchard.

Left and right were the rooms. I tell of them because long before we ever saw them in the flesh we knew just how they looked and they stood to us for America. On the left as one entered was the parlor, a cool, dark room, furnished in horsehair furniture, bookcases, and a lovely rosewood center table. There was a piano, too, and on the piano violins and a flute. Upon the walls hung etchings and pen and ink drawings of real beauty that Hermanus had made, and a landscape or two as well, and over the mantelpiece of carved and fluted white wood there was a dark oil portrait of Mynheer Stulting. A flowered carpet covered the whole floor, and long French windows opened to the garden.

To the right was the room where Hermanus slept for many years with his wife, only when I saw it the eldest son, Cornelius, had taken charge of the place and he and his wife lived in the room, and Hermanus, a straight-backed, fastidious little old gentleman with an astonishingly silvery and shining head of white hair, lived in the room next it down the hall, from whence, if the door were opened, one could hear the ticking of multitudinous clocks and huge old watches with which Hermanus was tinkering. Hermanus came out of that room every morning punctually at eight, although the family breakfasted at seven. When I first saw him come out thus he was already eighty-seven years of age, but carefully dressed and very upright in bearing, and his thick, upstanding white hair was brushed back from a low, square brow exactly like Carie's. He passed with a courteous, albeit somewhat militant, good morning to the dining room, which was at the further end of the hall and looked at one end into the vegetable garden and along its windowed length into the orchard. It was a cool, bare room, long in shape and with a few pieces of beautiful furniture and an oval table exquisitely carved.

This table explains the delight with which Carie once seized upon an oval table in an old second-hand shop in Shanghai. There had been an auction somewhere the day before, the greasy Chinese proprietor explained, and he had bought the table from a ship's captain, an Englishman, who told him the table was made of teak wood, shipped from India to England and made into a table by English workmen. From there the captain had brought it on his ship to his home in Shanghai, but when his wife died he sold his goods and so it fell into the hands of this Chinese dealer, and stood there in his small dusty shop, gracious and full of distinction, among heaps of rattan and broken rope furniture and old split bamboo stuff. Carie bought it for a few dollars and took it and polished it and doted on it, and thereafter it followed her about in her travels, although sometimes she lived in little upstairs rooms where the stairs were so narrow and so twisted the table could not pass through, and then it was lifted with ropes and coaxed through a window, swinging as it came over the narrow Chinese street, to the astonishment of paralyzed traffic in wheelbarrows and rikshas below it, and upturned yellow faces. But all the years I knew Carie she sat at the foot of this oval table, and I knew why, when I had seen the one in the dining room of the big house. By such links had she bound us bit by bit to her own country.

Up the wide stair of that house, mahogany stairs with a white handrail, there were six big square bedrooms, and the front one on the right-hand side was Carie's room. It looked out over the smooth wooded greenness of Little Levels to the distant mountains and immediately below it was the flower garden, and beyond, the big maple. In the room there were deep closets along one wall, deep enough for the hooped skirts Carie wore when she was a girl, and a window seat made into a hat box to hold her scoop bonnets. In the center of the room was her bed, wide, white, cool under its flowered muslin curtains. Upon the walls, papered with tiny sprays of pink roses and pale green ferns, were three pictures, a Madonna, very dim and old in a gilt frame that Hermanus had bought once in France, a daguerreotype of Carie's mother, and a print of a shepherd leading his sheep home in the evening, over a road winding between low hills. Carie always loved a shepherd leading his sheep. In her room in the mission house there was a picture of the same theme, cut from a magazine and framed with her own hands, and above the grave of her little children she had had carved the shepherd words, "He shall carry the lambs in his bosom." So this room of hers made me understand many little touches about that other house set remote on alien soil.

Upon the floor of this girlhood room there was a fresh straw-colored matting and over it a rose-flowered carpet. In the high windows were seats and there were ruffled white curtains with rose-colored loops. There were two chairs, one a white-painted rocking chair and one a ladder-backed straight chair with a reed bottom. There were a little rosewood dressing table and a bureau and above the table an oval mirror set in a carved, pale gilt frame. Somewhere there was always a bowl of flowers, a book open, a piece of sewing in progress. It was a room indescribably fragrant and simple and pure. I have put down its details because here it was she lived her own life, slept, and had her dreams.

On the third floor was the great attic, and the gabled windows looked over the level, lush meadows. Under the roof were trunks, small, hard, round-backed trunks that had come from Holland. There, too, were accumulating piles of *Godey Books* and *Pearson's Magazines,* and there boxes of old dresses and rags waiting to be braided into rugs. From the ceiling hung branches of dried herbs that the little French mother had taught them in her day to cull and to hang for the flavoring of soups and for making medicinal teas.

This attic was never hot. It stood high and, moreover, the air in the lofty, plain-like valley was always cool, even in summer. Often there were heavy, silvery mists, rising in the night and clinging in the hollows halfway to noon, and by sunset the air had a mountain chill to it again.

Having felt the vigor and surprise of that keen air, I marveled at the endurance which Carie had shown in those years of sickly summer heat and hot and fetid autumns. Bred in this sparkling and cool sunshine, in these pure and silvered mists of America, it was no wonder that sometimes she fainted in the thick sultriness of an August noon in a southern Chinese city, filled too full of human breath and of the odor of sweating human flesh.

But on this clear plain, in its swift mists and sharp winds and sunshine, she grew stronger and lithe in her youth. There were acres to run over; animals to care for and fondle; cows in the barn, deep-eyed, lowing, fruitful; horses to ride and to feed sugar and apples; chickens and turkeys to herd over the field of stubble when the grain had been cut, so that they might catch the grasshoppers springing everywhere. There was the life in the home, the house full of children, the busy, chirping little mother, the delicate, fastidious father, the grave, kindly elder brother. Everyone was busy and happy, and there were evenings spent in music, when one played the violin, another the flute, another the piano, and they sang together.

Once I said to Carie, "What do you remember out of the earliest years most clearly?"

Her eyes sparkled and softened as she rememberd, then flashed again. "Once when I was three years old I remember wanting to help my little mother who was washing the dishes. I lifted a big, blue-patterned meat dish from the table. It was one Grandfather had brought in the old days from Holland. I carried it slowly and carefully to put it away in the closet in the dining room, and it was so big I could not see over it to the floor. There was a board sticking up just a little and I was barefoot and stubbed my toe, and down I went, a fat, heavy little girl, on top of that blue dish, and smashed it to bits. I remember my father whipped me for it on the spot and I cried dreadfully, not because the whipping hurt, but because I had not meant to do anything but help. I never feel to this day that I should have had that whipping.

Even now, when I am fifty years old, I feel the injustice still!"

She was rolling out a great, soft, spongy mass of bread on the kitchen table as she talked. There in her Chinese kitchen she used to make her own bread, turning out big, brown, sweet loaves and little, crisp, southern rolls. The window was open and from the street below a clangor of cymbals arose from some procession passing and in the clangor there was twisted the thin, wiry wailing of a flute. I went idly to see what it was about, and there was an idol procession passing—not a very large procession and the idol not a great one, evidently, for he sat very small and drooping in his sedan chair, a little earthen figure in tattered paper robes. Ahead of him was a ragged priest with the cymbals and behind the chair were two more priests, one of them blowing disconsolately on the flute. The third priest carried a wooden drum shaped like a fish head, and this he struck occasionally, when he thought of it, with a wooden mallet. The street crowd scarcely lifted their heads to look at the procession, but behind ran perseveringly a small crowd of boys to see what could be seen.

She kneaded her bread, but she was ten thousand miles away. Then she said, "Well, but it was a happy life in that home. As far back as I can remember—do you suppose that crazy flute reminds me?—we had the house somehow full of music. The older ones all played something and we little ones sang. Cornelius was a good singing teacher. Years later at the seminary when I had the best singing teacher to be had, she couldn't teach me much that was new. Cornelius had already taught me how to let my voice flow out in a stream. We used to sing the "Messiah." How I remember it!"

And lifting her hands from the dough, she stood simply and sang the Hallelujah Chorus, her throat full and quivering. The Chinese cook dropped a pan he held and stared at her, and then went doggedly to his pans again, able to make nothing of it, but accustomed now to hearing her burst into singing suddenly. The clanging of the

31

cymbals faded into the noise of the street and watching her I could see her standing in the choir loft of the white frame American church that later took the place of the first log building. When I was there many years later the apple trees pressed against the open windows and filled the church with their scent. That day there was in the choir a young girl, Cornelius's daughter, and she sang like this, but her voice was not so great and thrilling as this woman's here in the Chinese city.

Suddenly she stopped, and the air of the kitchen seemed pulsing with the echoes of her voice, and she turned back to her bread. "Well," she said after a while, "it was a happy life until the Civil War came. What a time that was!"

What a time indeed! When the war broke out the Stulting family was in the section of Virginia which went with the North and became West Virginia. By this time Hermanus was no longer a young man. He was forty years old, a frail, stiff, upright figure, his hair already a silvery pompadour above his finely lined face. The little French wife was showing signs, too, of a life harder than she should have had. She was shrunken to a tiny figure, and there were evident the seeds of the tuberculosis that later was to carry her life away. Cornelius was a man of twenty, old for his years, a patient young man, extremely wise and gentle in his manner, dark-eyed, dark-haired, devoted to books and to music. But he had put his hand to the land and he had accepted it as a necessity that the burden of the family must fall upon him rather than upon his father. Strange magic personality of Hermanus, that even though he never shared in the drudgeries of their life, even though his fastidiousness had too early put burdens upon his older children, yet they all worshipped him and united to keep him the city gentleman he was by birth! Did it ever occur to Cornelius as a lad, when he struggled into his stiff work clothes at dawn, that his father lay sleeping and would sleep another three hours until they had all breakfasted and that even then his chocolate would be carried to his room that he might drink it before he dressed? Once I asked this of Carie and she said, "I suppose he satisfied something in our lives in those days. We all loved fine and beautiful things and there was not much left after the war. But none of us ever questioned our father. We just took it for granted from our mother that he was not strong enough for the hard work and it must not be asked of him. He always managed the bees and pruned the grapevines and the rose trees. He had a wonderful way with the bees, and we always had delicious honey. I don't believe he was ever stung in his life. He had a delicate way with him, and he had the cleverest, most dexterous hands I ever saw. And no bit of beauty ever escaped him. There was a white grapevine that grew against the barn, and I can remember now how the great white bunches looked in among the dewy green leaves. He always made us come to see them before he cut them. He said they were like moon agates for beauty. I suppose that is why we loved him—because he made us see beauty.

"Yes, of course Cornelius was really the man of the family. I know he and our mother always talked over the family accounts and how to spend the money well. As early as I can remember I always went to him for everything I needed. Of course it meant he could not marry when we were all little. I don't remember that he even looked at a girl then. He did not marry until after we were all grown and long after the war.

"But still our father stood for something to us. We were not common farming folk like the people around us. We always had books and music and our father's painting and jewelry work. Father stood for the difference. I remember being mightily proud because my father wore a black coat and changed his white shirt and collar every day and none of our neighbors did. It did not occur to me until years later that, after all, there was something cruel about those white collars. Someone—our mother as long as she could and then one of the older girls—always had that collar and shirt to wash and iron every day, no

33

matter how much canning or churning there might be on hand."

When the war broke, therefore, it came to be a matter for sharp fear as to what they would do if Cornelius had to fight. He was determined not to volunteer. Hermanus had taught them all to have a horror of slavery, and even in a neighborhood where many of the wealthier people owned slaves, when their land needed labor, Hermanus would buy no slaves. Some insistence on freedom, inherent in his blood, cried out to abstain from buying human beings to compel them to his will. If he used negro labor he paid for it scrupulously with money and he would not own anyone. All the children caught from him this passion for freedom, and when the war called there was nothing to challenge them to give up Cornelius to fighting for the South. At the same time their loyalties were enough to the South so that it was intolerable to think of fighting against Virginia. Neutrality, therefore, a thing difficult in the best of times, now became the only possible course open to them, and Hermanus and Cornelius declared themselves neutral. It was not a stand that tended to make them popular in the heat of the hour, but this Hermanus at least did not mind. Indeed, his was the temperament that thrived best on opposition, and I have heard that at this time he marched with a little extra grandeur and an exaggerated erectness of carriage to the church, and with a slight additional arbitrariness in his manner he set the tunes for the psalms. There was some threatening murmur against him, especially among slave owners, but such was his known integrity and such his fearlessness and haughtiness that no one was openly against him.

But with Cornelius, a young man, it was a different matter. When he was approached to join one side or the other, he replied that his mother and little brother and sisters depended on him for their living and if he left there would be no one to look after them. He bore with patience and in silence the taunts he heard in the village and he set himself steadily to his fields.

Nevertheless, as time went on and the scarcity of men on the southern side became acute, he had to think of some way to avoid impressment. At first they had not believed it possible that he would be actually seized and forced into the army. But this happened. One day when he came in at noon there were a few soft-voiced, steely-eyed southern soldiers in grey uniforms waiting for him and they followed him into the house. One of them said, "Reckon you'll have to fight, son, whether you want to or not. We have to find men."

"You will have to take me by force then," replied Cornelius simply, gazing back at them.

"Well, force, then," said the soldier, and he turned to his men. "Bind him and set him on the horse!"

The three other soldiers stepped forward and tied his wrists together and led him outside and tossed him on the waiting horse. The little French mother had been out in the garden picking beans and the screams of the children fetched her and she saw instantly what was happening. She rushed to her son's side and clung to his leg.

"You must let him go—he is the breadwinner!" she cried, panting.

The soldier touched his cap. "Sorry, ma'am—orders!"

"No—no—no—you must let him go—he is my son!"

"Forward—march!" said the soldier abruptly, and they mounted their horses and swung into line, and the little woman began to run, clinging to her son's leg. He leaned over in alarm to whisper to her, "I'll find a way back, Mother. Don't—you can't keep up. I'll desert—"

"Yes, and be shot for it!" she whispered back fiercely. "No, I'll never let you go."

She ran faster as the horse broke into a canter, and at last was half dragged over the ground, but she would not let go. The soldier in charge could not endure the sight. He stopped to argue with her.

"Ma'am, there isn't a bit of use in this. He's got to go. It's orders. I'm right sorry, ma'am, but everywhere sons have got to fight."

"Not mine!" she gasped determinedly. Her sunbonnet

was hanging down her back, and her curly grey hair was shaken down and hung all about her little thin face. Her eyes were staring with fatigue and her throat throbbing and her bosom bursting with her heavy pants. "If he goes—I go—too. Besides—we don't believe—in slavery. Isn't freedom—what our country stands for?—Are you—going to make him fight—for—for what we don't believe in?"

The soldier looked at her. Then he gave the orders again, somewhat half-heartedly, "Forward, march!"

Again the horse broke into a canter and he tried not to see the small, brown-clad figure, gasping and clinging to the young man's leg, her feet half tripping, half swinging, over the rough road. Her lips were parted in dreadful gasps, and her brown eyes stared ahead in agony. Her son bent over her crying in a low voice, "Mother—mother—mother—"

It was too much. The soldier let her run thus for a mile, and then he stopped, dismounted, took off his cap, and bowed.

"Ma'am, you have the victory. He is yours." And then to the men he said, "Take off his ropes and let him go."

In a moment the mother and son stood alone in the road and in the distance the horsemen rode away with one horse riderless. Cornelius looked at his mother with unspeakable tenderness and she flashed her eyes and began to gather up her hair in her trembling hands. Then she grew faint and leaned against him and whispered out of parched lips, "I just wasn't going to have it!"

But it was a lesson to them of what might happen again. Another officer might not be so lenient with them as this one. They must hide Cornelius. So he left the house that night and went on horseback with a little roll of bedding and a basket of food and he rode away to the mountain in the distance, Droop Mountain, it was called, and there in a little hollow, cup-like valley at its summit was an empty, ruined cabin and a deserted meadow or two.

Here the young man lived alone for the two years until

the war ended. The land he dug and planted with beans and corn and wheat, and when there were harvests he stole back by night to his home to take them food and to see his mother and get what he needed for himself. When the Little Levels was swept by the passing and repassing of northern and southern armies, when fields were devastated and barns and stores robbed, these meager harvests that Cornelius brought were the mainstay of the family, and often all they had to depend upon for food. I purposely do not put into this period of Carie's life that is occupied by the Civil War those things one may find in any book of its history. I put what she told me, a little American girl, alien in the Chinese city, and seeing America through her eyes, and enthralled with her stories of my own country, the country I had never seen.

War I knew perfectly well. At this time we white people in China were living through the uncertainties and possibilities of the Boxer Rebellion. Every night my clothes were put beside my bed so that I might slip into them instantly if the call came to escape. Carie taught me how to place them, how to tie my shoes most swiftly, how to seize my hat from the floor beside the chair as I went, lest we have to walk by day under the poisonous Oriental sun. I had to do this for myself, for there was another younger than I who could not see to herself. A basket of canned milk stood ready day and night for the baby. It stood by the door, where in passing and in haste it might be caught up. Carie was prepared in every detail, ready, fearless, not allowing us to be afraid. We knew she would take care of us.

This fearlessness she had learned, beyond what was native to her intrepid nature, during those four years of the Civil War when she was a little girl. During the long, hot summer of 1900 we used to beg her, "Tell us stories of our own war in America!" And she recreated for us the stirring days, told from the viewpoint of a little girl in the highlands of West Virginia, the borderland between North and South, where both armies swept back and forth in the struggle. Afterwards when I had to study this period in history, it was already learned from her, immeasurably more vivid, more full, than any book could make it for me.

I caught from her the spirit of great movements of armies, at first gay and assured, then shaken, surprised, bitter, then vengeful and desperate, and at last despairing and vanquished. More dreadful even than these were the armies of the victors, sweeping triumphant over the fertile fields, devastating conquerors.

Once she said, her eyes dark with memory, "The Yankees used to shout at us that Sherman said he was going to lay a track straight to Georgia so wide and so bare that a crow couldn't find a grain of corn. I reckon he did it, too." Again she said, with much simplicity, "Sherman said war was hell. Well, he ought to know by now whether it is so or not. He's been there for a good many years."

Or again she said, "Not that any of my family believed in slavery. We didn't, any more than Lincoln did. We were Americans and we couldn't see slaves in America and think it right. But that's no way to free slaves—to let a lot of them all loose at once. Why, after the war we hardly dared to stir abroad, and we didn't have many negroes in our section, either. I remember Brother Cornelius had to join the Ku Klux Klan for a while to get the freed slaves to leave us alone."

Once she laughed suddenly and sat down and laughed until her eyes were wet. "I never shall forget one morning when the Yankees had been camping overnight in the orchard. It was winter and the trees were bare. I went out to look at the men from behind the barn, because I'd heard so many things of them—people in our parts said they had horns like devils. Well, when I went out the trees were just full of curious-looking fruit. I couldn't imagine what it was and I went closer to see, and they were cakes of bread! The men had been served up cakes made of sour corn meal and they wouldn't eat them and they threw them up into the trees for sport until the branches were full of them. The funniest sight! But the birds fed there for months."

"Did the Yankees have horns?" I asked, breathless.

"They did not," she declared, her eyes twinkling. "They were just like anybody else, and I was fearfully disappointed."

This was one of our favorite stories, and we asked for it again and again. One day Hermanus heard that a Yankee army was coming. He happened at that time to have in his house some very fine old jewels he was resetting which belonged to a wealthy landed family near by. He was exceedingly anxious lest he be robbed of them, and their value was far above anything he could repay. He decided, therefore, to hide them, and he put them into a small covered basket and carried them to the meadow adjacent to the garden and thrust them far under a large flat stone there. In the afternoon the Yankees came and to his horror chose as their camping spot that very meadow. They sat upon the stone, used it as a table, at night pitched a tent over it. From his window Hermanus could see it all. As long as daylight lasted he kept watch at the window to see whether anyone stooped to look under it. By dusk it still seemed safe as far as could be seen. But after dark, although great torches flared, the shadows cast such uncertain shapes that none could be sure what happened.

Hermanus walked the floor that night, praying and commanding them all to pray, and all the while he blamed himself for not returning the jewels to the owner and tried confusedly to think what he would do if they were lost, for the owner was a proud man and notoriously hard and exacting and these were family jewels and quite irreplaceable. When dawn came the armies moved on and Hermanus ran out sick with anxiety. He stopped to look under the stone. There the little basket of jewels stood, just as he had left it, safe and unseen. At this happy conclusion of the tale, which Carie made the more exciting with her lowered voice and widened eyes and vivid face, we all drew a deep breath. Usually she told the stories in the evening when we sat on the veranda at the end of the day, and we looked out over the paddy fields and the thatched roofs of the farmers in the valley, and in the distance a slender pagoda seemed to hang against the bamboos on a hillside. But we saw none of these. We saw as clearly as though we were there the rougher fields and more rugged mountainsides of our own country, and over them the dashing horses and the streaming flags of the men in blue and grey.

Then there was the dreadful day when North and South met in the battle of Droop Mountain, and all day and all night the cannon roared back and forth over the mountain and the family sat in fear, scarcely able to pray, even, lest Cornelius be caught in his hiding place. But before dawn he staggered in, his hands and clothing torn and his bare legs badly scratched. He had hidden in a cave through the day and in the cover of darkness he had run down the steep cliff-like side of the mountain. He was alive and unhurt, but his little field, ploughed ready for seed, was ruined by cannon shells.

There was the day when there was nothing in the house to eat at all except a quart measure full of dried beans and on that day also came a desperate little band of fugitive southern soldiers, ragged, barefoot, starving. The little mother seeing them, cooked all the store of beans and there was a bowlful of soup and beans for each, and that afternoon the children went out to hunt for dandelion greens for supper.

These stories and many others she told to us during the hot summer days outside the Chinese city. All about us there seethed hatred of us who were foreign, but I did not know it. Listening to her, I saw my own country and the heroism of my own people, and it fortified me. She had not been afraid. She had learned even as a little child to look on wounded and bleeding men and not faint, to endure hunger and make the best of it, to think of some resource when there seemed to be none, and all this was glorified by the high spirit of the hour.

She was eight years old when the Civil War ended and

40

her family, as did all the others in the township, had to settle themselves to new conditions. When defeat was accepted, a fever to begin life was everywhere present. During these four years there were no schools. Carie taught herself to read, asking of this one and that what this letter and the other was. But except for reading she knew nothing. The little sister just younger than she could not even read.

There were many other children in the same plight, for parents had been too distraught, fathers fighting desperately, mothers doing farm work and carrying on business and striving to take the place of both mother and absent father. Now the thought of all was that somehow schools must be started to repair the waste of the war years.

Cornelius, feeling keenly the ignorance of his brother and sisters, was the first in the town to organize a school. He taught it himself, doing what farm work he could in the early morning and at night after he came home. The school started in one room under the church but it grew rapidly and later moved into its own building and one day came to be known as The Academy.

To Carie it was the gate of life. She had been impatient these two years and more for learning, for knowledge to help her understand many things about which she had begun to wonder. She was a strange child in certain ways, imaginative, passionate, sensitive to the point often of suffering, a strange compound of fiercely practical common sense and profound mysticism. She used to lie out under the stars at night, barelegged in the deep grass of the meadow in front of the white house, and looking deep into the sky she thought of the stars and of what they were and ached with her longing to fathom the universe. Stars always had a fascination for her. I remember on the hot nights of summer in the Chinese city she would lean out of the window above the noisome street and look to the stars hanging heavy and golden out of the blackly purple sky and say, "It is hard to believe they are the same stars I used to see as a little girl in the meadow. They looked cool and silvery there and infinitely far and ethereal.

41

Here they seem solid and sultry and too near. I used to dream there were people on them—transparent, delicate fairy folk. But here one feels that humans live on them —hot, wicked people. Look at red Orion hanging there on the pagoda top!"

In the village school she learned her first astronomy, a subject always favorite with her except that she was somewhat dashed by the mathematics. She had a vivid imagination that laid hold on every dry fact and gave it substance and life. Cornelius was a born teacher and she an apt pupil, not facile of memory so much as of understanding and quick of comprehension, so that between these two there was not only the bond of brother and sister, but of loved pupil and passionately revered teacher.

The post-war period in the life of the little West Virginia town was one of deep spiritual fervor coupled with necessarily ascetic living. This atmosphere was the air which she breathed in her youth, and which forever placed a check upon a nature that was at heart sensuous and beauty-loving. But it gave also the opportunity for experience of many sorts and in this her varied mind delighted. I remember her saying once, "I have done every kind of work needed to maintain life and I am glad of it. After the Civil War there were no shops, nothing to be bought. We grew our own flax and we spun linen thread and made our own sheets and table cloths and inner clothing. We dyed our dresses from cotton and linen thread we had made ourselves and we wove it. I learned to know what colors could be made from different herbs and barks and from roots of many kinds. Sometimes our experiments were failures and we had to wear them just the same. And we sheared sheep and washed the wool and carded it and spun it and wove it. I am glad I learned how to do everything."

They had to make even the hoops they wore in their skirts and these they made from the long withes of the greenbrier bushes. These did well enough until they dried and snapped. I remember asking over and over for a story that she never failed to tell with merry eyes as she told it.

"How my hoop snapped? Well, one Sunday I went to church—of course we had to go every Sunday—but this Sunday there was a missionary speaking and the little church was very full and dear good Mrs. Dunlop, the minister's wife, sat next to me. She was a darling and I loved her but she was very fat and she kept squeezing against me so that it seemed to me she just expanded more and more. It was a hot summer's day, too. Well, she kept expanding and she pushed against my hoop, and at last my hoop—it wasn't a big one, really, because my father wouldn't let us wear very big ones—but my hoop just rose up in front of me and lifted my skirt shamefully high, and I tried to press it down and it wouldn't go down. Well, at last I grew desperate because a boy was sitting just behind and I could hear him snickering, so I gave a good hard push and there was a loud snap. My greenbrier hoop! My skirt went down all of a sudden then, but you should have seen me when I stood up. My skirt hung about me and it was so long it trailed on the ground. Good Mrs. Dunlop stood in front of me and I walked out to the buggy behind her and climbed in right quick. Afterwards we laughed and laughed, but I was dreadfully ashamed that day, although I couldn't keep from laughing too. I knew I looked funny. Father said it was a judgment on me for vanity. Maybe it was, but I always felt it was because the greenbrier was just too dry and couldn't stand the strain of Mrs. Dunlop's expansion!"

To us little American children in the Chinese city nothing was more stirring in all the absorbing tale of her life in our country than the story of maple sugar. In the home at that time after the war everything that could be made was made and nothing bought except the chocolate Hermanus must have in the morning and coffee and tea.

To this day I have never been to a sugaring, nor even seen a tree pierced for its sweet water, but I have had the spiritual experience. I had it over and over again in that Oriental country where a sugar maple never grew except in our dreams. But I know that in the chill beginning of early spring, when indeed spring is more a hope than a fact, you must go about and tap the great trees that were golden in the autumn. And that means you make a little hole and stick a wooden tube called a spile in it and set a bucket below and the sweet water runs into it. Then when the buckets are full and enough water has collected you gather it all together and pour it into the great iron cauldron at the sugaring camp. The boys have chopped wood and the kettle is hung on a rude crane and the fire is lit and the water starts boiling.

Then is the time for fun, for all the boys and girls of the town gather at the sugar camp and watch the sugaring and take a hand at the stirring and put great logs under the pot, and if there is snow as there ought to be, there is tobogganing between times and games and laughter. Everybody's cheeks are crimson and all eyes are bright and there is fun everywhere.

When the syrup is thick enough to make maple syrup it is poured into great kegs and is mated to buckwheat cakes and waffles and pancakes for the rest of the year, but if you want sugar you must boil the sweet water longer and it takes an old hand to know just when the right moment comes to pour the hot stuff into little shapes and big ones.

Great round molds made the big cakes of sugar that were kept for household use through the year but there were many hundreds of little heart-shaped tins and star shapes and crescents and many others and these were filled, too. Best fun and most delicious of all was to pour the hot sugar out on snow and eat it suddenly cooling and scoop up the handfuls of snow and stiffening hot sugar. Then when it was all finished and the sugaring over, everybody went home singing through the sharp sweet air, and no one was ever sick from eating so much—as much as one wanted. That was because it was so clean in the woods where the camp was and the pure cold snow covered everything and the air was keen and made one strong and robust enough for anything. Ah, Carie, how you made us dream of our country!

Snow! How she made us see snow in America! Sometimes, once in a long time, we had a little drift of it in the southern Chinese city where we lived, sometimes on a chilly, damp, wintry day. We pressed our faces against the windowpane and watched it coming down, white against the grey sky, melting instantly as it touched the warmer black tiles of the roofs. Once I remember there was a corner in the courtyard where the wind had blown a tiny drift as faint as a mist, but still made of snow. We went running out, leaping and crying, "Snow—snow!" Ono winter of unprecedented cold, real snow came down outside the city wall and there on the barren gravelands there was at least an inch of snow and if one did not look too closely at the stubble sticking through, the world looked white and clean. The bamboos were feathery dusty with snow and the small new wheat stood freshly green between white patches of graves. Carie nailed together some boards from a box that had held canned milk and tied a grass rope to it and we slid down steeply sloping Chinese graves on the contrivance and dreamed of tobogganing in America.

Years later when I saw real snow in deep Virginian woods in the Blue Mountains, I knew that spiritually I had seen it all before because of what this American woman had told me. I saw meadows hidden, still and sleeping under it. I saw roofs under great blankets of it and windows peering out, cozy and merry, from beneath, and smoke curling against the still sky. It was all just as she had said. Before I had turned a corner of the road that led into the hills, my heart cried that the shadows on the snow would be blue under the lee of the hills, and when I turned, there blue shadows lay. She had shown them to me ten years before and ten thousand miles away, so that I knew them.

All this beauty of her country went into these years of her life between her earliest childhood and her twenty-third year, when she went away. If the great gift from her father was to show her where beauty lay, she needed little showing, for she had seeing eyes. Wide beauty of meadow and valley and mountain, of the seasons of the year each in its time, these she saw with unfailing response; but small beauties she saw as quickly, little beauties of close-set moss and small flowers and insects. Once she bent over a colored spider, gay in red and black, and at last put out a small finger to feel the color, and the spider stung her and her whole arm swelled from the poison. Thereafter she only looked, but it was characteristic of her sense of fair play to remember that after all she had provoked the insect, and its beauty was not marred for her.

This love of beauty and instant response to it, then, was part of her very blood and bone, and emotion and abandon to beauty was always a part of her. She could go drunk in a sunlit meadow on a spring day, laughing and sparkling and all but dancing. But she loved the beauty of clean, simple, steady things as well. There was for her beauty not only in a pool of mountain water under moonlight, but as well in a room made still and clean and fresh, in dishes newly washed and shining. I remember her saying that one of her pleasures in the austere times after the Civil War was that there were no new dishes to be bought and so every day they had to use the blue and white willow-pattern china and the thin crystal wine goblets that her grandparents had brought from Holland. Every day she chose to wash them, above every other household task, so that she might feel their delicacy in her hands. This remained to her a memory of beauty all the days of her life.

Hers was a sensuous nature. She loved the feel of things, the textures of silk and porcelain and linen and velvet, the touch of rose leaves, the roughness of pine cones. I can remember her taking into her hands the smooth, dry stiffness of a bamboo leaf and rubbing it. "So hard and smooth and fine," she murmured. She had an abnormally keen sense of smell. One of the tortures of her life in the Orient was the stink of manure and of human filth that pervaded the garden from outside the city wall, where nightsoil from the city was the chief fertilizer used to force the earth to rich and rapid fruitage.

I remember forever the first time she came back to her own country. She would stand knee deep in a meadow or perhaps in a wood and draw one great breath after another, or else she would take little quick sniffs, little tastes of smell.

"What is it?" we cried, anxious to miss nothing, and her answer come back joyously, "Just smelling it all! Do you know, one of the loveliest things about this America of ours is its smell—its lovely, lovely *smell!*"

She liked to take a handful of pine needles and rub them in her hands and hold them to her nostrils, and she would grow drunken with the pine fragrance, her eyes closed in ecstasy. But it was such scents she loved, pure, pungent odors, or the frail fragrance of a tea rose. Many of the Oriental flowers she rejected because she disliked their heavy, musky sweetness.

Of music she had a good, intellectual understanding, but music remained for her always primarily a sensation and an emotion. In the years when I was an impatient adolescent it was annoying to me that she could not hear great music without having the tears stream down her cheeks, not tears of pain, primarily, but tears that were response from a heart too finely strung and too sensitive to bear unmoved the beauty of music. In the arrogance of my youth I said, "If you cannot keep from crying, why will you persist in going to hear it?"

She gave me one of her deep, steady looks and at last she replied, "You don't understand now. How can you? You have not had time for life yet. Some day you will listen and hear that music is not technique and melody, but the meaning of life itself, infinitely sorrowful and unbearably beautiful. Then you will understand."

There was in her great love of color a curious contradiction. She chose always delicate and finely shaded tones. I have pondered much over this, for in her nature were a passion and a wildness which seemed to me to call for

47

the more barbaric hues, and I have a theory, whether true or not, that in the instinctive choice of colors people most truly reveal themselves. The reds and yellows of old imperial China were always distasteful to her. I think there was an abandon there which frightened her—an abandon to the flesh. I think it frightened her because she felt something too passionate in her own blood and she was fearful of her own response. No, she chose for her favorite shades the pale, cool, rosy yellow of a tea rose that grew beside the veranda steps—an American tea rose, and she loved also the warm delicacy of old-fashioned salmon pinks. Later when her hair was white and she took to wearing gowns of silvery grey, there was always a touch somewhere of one or the other of these shades. I think she knew that in herself there was a certain pagan quality, a passion, a temper too vigorous and lusty, and the puritan strain of her blood and of her training in her times warred sternly against it.

If she could come from the lonely grave where she lies I think she would not like those words I have just written. She would look at me troubled and say, "Did I not struggle all my life against these very things you are telling about me now that I am dead?" And I would answer, if I could, "Ah, yes, we saw the struggle, but do you not know we loved you for the very things in yourself that you hated?"

For when we think of her and talk of her we always feel her as two distinct persons. One is this warm, merry, sensuous, hot-tempered person; a woman quick to see the ridiculous, a born actress and mimic, making us all laugh when she was in one of her funny moods and took to copying the voice and gait and manners of someone; sweeping us all up in a chorus of gay song, dropping work all of a sudden on a summer's day to go off to a garden or a mountain for a picnic. The other is the puritan, the practical mystic, straining after God but never quite seeing Him, always planning further hours for prayer, for deeper consecration, more devotion, but never quite achieving what she planned, and from that very sense of religious failure, more passionately rigid with herself on the other side, the passionate and emotional side, that she had been taught was wicked and would lead her away from God. There was a continual war in her members.

When I meditate on the period of her life that formed her, I begin to understand this conflict inherent in her very nature. From Hermanus she had the love of beauty that was inseparable from her being. From her good Dutch grandparents she had the practical determination that would not let her rest—a power for sacrifice for righteousness' sake was in her very blood. She had been bred on the story of leaving all and forging forth into a new country for God's sake. She came of pilgrim stuff. But there was in this already incongruous mixture the gay, practical, none-too-religious heart of the little French mother, who loved passionately, not God but first Hermanus and her children and then for their sakes the good God.

Yet in other years, when I knew better my own country and its people, I knew Carie better, too. In this very disunity, in the richness of her variety, sprung from the dissimilar sources of her blood, from her pioneer heritage, from the swift and elemental experiences of her life, she was the more America.

For in spite of all the happiness of the life of the big square house, in spite of music making and school and parties in the village, Carie was not always happy. Perhaps no one in her times was ever quite happy, because there was always the matter of one's soul.

In her most joyful moments she remembered her soul. Sometimes at the height of fun, with her friends listening to her joking and teasing and laughing, she would be stopped suddenly, as though a cold hand were laid upon her heart, and she thought in a panic, "What about my eternal soul?" Sometimes when she worked about the house and stopped a moment to look through the open door into the garden and to wonder if heaven could be more beautiful, the sharp fear rushed into her mind, "But I am not saved—will I see heaven?"

It was very hard not to think of such things. Long church services on Sunday, prayers twice a day at home, the minister's gentle penetrating questions, the desire of the father and mother to see each child "saved" and joined to the church all kept her from being quite happy.

But it was never fear of hell which drove Carie into trying to find God. Indeed, I never saw her afraid of anything, and I do not for a moment believe anyone could have drawn a hell fearful enough to compel her against her will. No, she wanted passionately to be good. She used to say to us often, "It is so beautiful to be good, child—be good, because it is the loveliest thing on earth." She wanted to find God because that was the only way, they told her, to be good. One's own goodness was all "filthy rags," the Bible said, unless one found God.

She told me once that the years of her adolescence were miserable with the restlessness of this search. One after the other of the more facile-hearted of her friends was "converted" and took communion. But Carie, sitting mutinous and agonizing in the little church, shook her head above the bread and wine. She would not deceive herself or anyone. She had prayed and prayed.

In her diary I find written of this time: "During the years between twelve and fifteen I used many times a week to go out into the woods behind the barn and creep into a little hollow in a clump of elderberries and throw myself down and cry to God for a sign—anything to make me believe in Him. Sometimes I vowed I would not, like Jacob, leave the spot until He gave me a sign for myself. But it never came. The tinkle of cowbells told me it was evening and the cows were coming home to be milked, and I must go and lay the table."

Over and over again she took her trouble to her Sunday school teacher, Mrs. Dunlop, the minister's wife, and the gentle placid woman tried to bring this passionate honest heart "through to salvation."

"Just give yourself to God, my dear—that's all it is,"

she said, filled with affection for the dark, downright girl she never quite understood. "Surely it is a very easy thing to give your heart to God."

But Carie must have more than this. "I want to feel God accepts me," she cried. "I can give myself, but why doesn't He accept me? Why doesn't He give me a sign?"

This was beyond old Mrs. Dunlop. She could only repeat patiently, "Just give yourself—just give yourself, dear!"

These were stormy years for Carie. Often her despair in not being able to be sure of God led her into opposite moods of recklessness and a gayety too wild for happiness. Sometimes, realizing with horror the tumult in her young blood, she felt herself hopelessly wicked. She grew frightened at the beginning of desire in herself.

She was a dark, handsome girl at this time, mature for her years, keen of humor and ready to laugh, and yet grave in her times of gravity. She had red lips and blooming cheeks and a mass of natural chestnut brown curls hanging over her head in a "waterfall."

The exact experience that came to her at this time I do not know, for she never told anyone. I only know that somewhere during these years she fell passionately in love with the handsome boy with a rollicking, beautiful voice, who had once laughed at her in church when her hoop snapped. He had grown to be a young man, tall and blond and debonair, who rejoiced somewhat at being among the "unbelievers," but who came to church for the singing, and, I am fain to believe, for Carie's sake. And they met at singing school too, one evening a week.

"He could sing the heart out of anyone," said Carie unwillingly, her eyes sober. This she said when she was grey-haired, but I could see in her eyes her memory hot still with the thought of him. Beyond this she told us nothing. I think his big fair body spoke to her warm blood intolerably and the puritan in her was mortally afraid of him. Whether he loved her long or not I do not know.

That he saw her with special eyes I know, for she would

acknowledge when pressed that he was "nice" to her and that she had to "make him stop" because she didn't want to marry him.

"Why not?" we demanded, for he sounded romantic.

"Because—because—he was not good. He drank and he came of a family that drank. It wasn't easy to be good, and I was afraid if I married him I might grow like him."

Whether Carie could have held to this stand alone I do not know. But this happened to be the year her little mother fell ill and Carie was seized out of the youthful life of her world to spend day and night at the side of death. There, watching her mother slip away, she vowed always to choose good rather than evil, to follow the stern side of herself rather than the gay, and all her life long to war against the sensuousness that she knew only too well to be in her blood. She would be good; she would deny herself to the uttermost; she would give herself to God. How could she deny herself most wholly? If she gave her whole life and self completely to God then perhaps He would give her a sign of His being and thus she could follow and find Him.

For in the sudden illness Carie forgot her own soul in a new terror. The mother had frankly loved Carrie better than all her other children. Carie could laugh so often with her. Carie was so quick with her hands. She was so good at cooking and so economical. She was the one, too, who loved herb gathering and gardening. And she was so strong. Sometimes she would seize her tiny mother and hold her high in the air like a child, and threaten not to let her down unless she would not work so hard or would eat more. "You big naughty girl," the little woman cried, pretending to be outraged, "you put me down—at once, I say! I am your mother!" But she loved it and leaned upon the girl. And Carie more than loved her mother. She gave her admiration and the two were free together, free that is, except in that dark quest for God. There Carie went alone, for the French mother could not understand the yearning in the daughter's heart. To go to church, to kneel when the father prayed, to keep a clean house and make the meals the best one could—it was enough for a woman. So Carie said nothing, and loved her mother tenderly because she was so childlike.

Now in her illness the mother became a child indeed, and clung to her daughter.

The illness had come so quickly. One winter's day the mother went into the cold cellar to fill a dish of pickles from a jar, and because the jar was empty stayed to open another, and took cold. It grew swiftly into racking coughs and then into a swift consumption. In spite of her refusal to believe her mother would die, Carie was too honest not to see the truth.

Not that she was daunted even by death. She went gallantly through everything. She was gay about the bed and she kept the sickroom sweet and shining and fresh with flowers, and she washed and starched and ironed the little frilled lace caps her mother wore, and made her pretty bed gowns and put all her pleasure in dressing dolls into the care of the little sunken-eyed woman in the big bed.

Hermanus at this time moved into another room and Carie slept beside her mother and warmed the little, frail, cold body with her robust youth, and made play of everything and would not let her mother be afraid.

But one night her mother fell into dreadful coughing and Carie ran to lift her head. Then her mother looked at her, sick and racked, and she moaned, "Child—is this —d-ea-th?" She would only spell the word.

Suddenly Carie could not bear the fear in her mother's eyes. Oh, if only she knew about God—if only she could say to her mother, "I *know*."

She must have a sign. . . . She would give herself. "I will give my whole self to God—my whole life," she whispered passionately. Her mind went searching recklessly ahead. There must be no half measures—no sacrifice that was not complete. "I will go as a missionary, surely I cannot give myself more than that."

Suddenly the end came. Her mother cried out faintly,

and Carie lifted her high in her arms. She saw her mother's dim eyes lighten. A faint smile of surprise broke over her white lips and she gasped, "Why—it's—all *true!*"

For a moment she gazed suddenly and clearly through the walls of the room into the space of some other world and then she died. Carie, hearing the cry, catching the gaze of her mother's eyes, felt her heart stop. *Was this God's sign?* In great awe she laid her mother gently down.

II

SO Carie vowed away her life. Steadfastly she set herself to the fulfillment. She missed her mother tragically.
She could never sing so light-heartedly now in the evenings because that small placid presence was gone, and
she held in her memory the hour when she had given
herself to God.

But still God gave no sign of acceptance. She must
wait until she saw what to do next, and meanwhile the
days must pass as they had before in work and school.
Only she was quieter and more steady. She refused to
join in the village parties. She would not go walking any
more with Neale Carter. She would study hard and fit herself for what she had promised to do.

The idea of missions was not new to her. Several times
there had come to the little village church gaunt sun-
burned men, missionaries to other lands, bringing their
burning words and stories. She listened, entranced against
her will, by gallant adventures for God's sake. But she
had not herself sought to find a "call." Why, it would

mean leaving America! She could not leave America. She always slipped out of the church gay with relief, avoiding the missionary's eyes.

Now all that was changed. She must be—she was—ready to go. She had promised. She went soberly about the house, but if anyone noticed it, it was only to say, "Carie feels her mother's death." But it was much more than that. She was beginning already to cut her life free, ready for a way to be shown her.

Two years passed by and Hermanus, as times prospered found his hobby becoming of practical use to him, for when the worst of the reconstruction days were over people from far and wide brought him clocks to mend and jewels to set. He made watches, also, and these were in great demand. There was some magic in his slender, agile fingers that charmed the most obdurate machinery to motion. For the first time in his life he contributed well to the family income.

Cornelius, however, was still the mainstay with his teaching and farming. The two older sisters held in their capable hands the management of the house and of the younger children. The great problem in the family was Luther, the younger son, the one most like Carie in nature and in appearance. But where in her there was a strong will toward self-control and a genuine desire for goodness, in him in his youth the flesh was dominant. He grew rebellious and wanted to go west where the gold fields at that time were luring every young man who had a drop of wanderlust in his veins. The family united in trying to hold him, but he had always loved his mother best and she understood him, and now when she was gone it was hard to keep him. Hermanus in a mighty passion wanted to whip him soundly, but the lad towered above him, a tall, black-eyed, black-haired young man, and the little, arrogant, militant father could not compass the deed for all his will to do it. Cornelius whipped him once at his father's command, and then threw down the whip in sickness of heart and would not again. Nothing seemed quite right since the mother died. But somehow the family life went on, and still Carie waited in intense secret determination.

By the time she was eighteen years old Dr. Dunlop, the minister of her childhood, was ready to retire, having grown fat and drowsy in the service. It was evident there must be a new minister. In this Hermanus took the lead as he did in all things in the village, and after many samplings and tastings of the various doctrines of the young men who came to preach trial sermons, a tall, grave man, young in years but bearing in his body the marks of premature age from his experience in the war, was chosen. He came from the same state and from the neighboring county of Greenbrier. His father was a leading landowner there, and after the war the young man had taught school, and then gone to seminary. From college and seminary he had come forth trailing clouds of *cum laudes,* with special mention of his amazing facility in languages, especially in Sanscrit, Arabic, Hebrew and Greek. There was a taste for liberal learning in the little village and Hermanus had the tradition of culture in his family and had maintained it well in his own generation. Moreover, the young minister was of pleasing appearance, tall, gentle, fair-haired, with a dainty little ruffled wife whom he carried on his arm like a pretty workbag. His trial sermon was doctrinally sound and he explained satisfactorily the traditional aspects of predestination and free will; also it was long and full of good meat and quite beyond the understanding of most of the younger members of the congregation. It was enough. He was the man.

That same summer after he had come to the village and had established himself in the creeper-grown manse next the white church, a younger brother who was still in college visited him, and this young man must be mentioned because of Carie. He was a student bent on the ministry, a tall, thin youth, with nearsighted blue eyes, vague and mystic in their gaze, a gentle voice and a mild smile. He was very shy and silent and steadfastly declined all invitations to join the choir or singing school. He replied, smiling, that he was very busy—that he was reading with his brother. Sundays he sat a little apart, seeming to see no one, on his face a look of rapt worship. Carie, if she looked at him, which she did not often, thought of him as an extremely saintly young man, lacking perhaps in a sense of humor, but certainly very good. Her own sense of humor was an everlasting cause of stumbling to her. It was shame to her that she could still see something funny even if it happened at a funeral, and more than once she had been overcome in church to her own confusion. And at such silly small things, too, she thought regretfully; as, for instance, when the flies would gather thick in the mass of tulle crowning little Miss Nelson's hat when she played the organ. There they immediately became caught in the folds of the stuff and set up a frantic buzzing and swarming, and under this confusion Miss Nelson, who was a small, shy, middle-aged lady, sat half fainting, her face scarlet with embarrassment. Once at least during the service she would escape between hymns and come back freed from the pest, but it would only be a short time before the sweetish starch in the tulle attracted more flies and they came sailing through the window, headed straight for her hat. Summer after summer it was a fly trap and a joke to the younger members of the congregation.

But the younger brother of the minister would not even see such a sight in church. His thoughts were elsewhere—doubtless only where they should be. Carie, feeling always humbled by the discrepancy between her achievements and her desires, was sobered by the very look of worship on the rugged, somewhat pale young face. But if she spoke to him that was all. He seemed a being apart because of his very nature and calling. She respected him mightily but gave him very little thought. Was there not a mission waiting for her?

When she was nineteen she had learned all that Cornelius could teach her and he was not willing that her swift and brilliant mind should stop with this. The family fortunes were recovered from the war, there was no special need for her at home, Luther had settled down and consented to go to school at last and "take an education," and Cornelius decided that Carie must be sent away to a young ladies' seminary and be given every opportunity to develop not only her mind but her powerful and beautiful voice.

It could not be an ordinary seminary. In addition to the curriculum of regular studies Hermanus demanded also that it be sound in religious doctrine, of Presbyterian foundation, and laying the emphasis on moral education and deportment. After considerable search the ideal place was found, Bellewood Seminary, near Louisville, Kentucky.

There Carie went in her nineteenth year, with a heart wildly excited. She had a new brown cashmere dress to travel in, and it was specially for the steamboat. It was made with a high bustle in the back and six ruffles round the bottom of the skirt, and there was cream lace ruffled in the bosom and at the cuffs. A small brown beaver hat trimmed in the same lace sat high on her curly hair. She was perfectly satisfied with her appearance, although she feared that her mouth was a trifle too large. But she had at that time the reddest possible lips and blooming pink cheeks. Once many years later her small daughter asked naïvely, "Mother, were you pretty when you were a girl?" Her golden brown eyes danced at this and she answered demurely, "Neale Carter seemed to think so when he saw me off to the Seminary!"

The next two years at Bellewood Seminary were happy ones, rich in friendships. There were seventeen girls in her class, and she became a leader among them, and won their love in a remarkable degree. Hers was a nature so large that she could comprehend in her heart any human being and she was always remarkable in the diversity of her friendships. The key to her instant interest was someone's need for love and help. I think Neale Carter more nearly won her on that score than on any other—that he needed her to make him good. At least once she told us he nearly had her on this plea, but her sharp and detached sense of humor discerned when next he fell—he was given to drinking—that he enjoyed a little too well the sinning and being forgiven, and so he lost her.

I have here beside me as relics of her school days two essays written in the beautiful spidery handwriting of those days. One is entitled *Queen Esther*. It is a dissertation on the sacrifice of the Jewish queen for her people —always that charm of self-sacrifice!—and on the giving of her life for them if it were needful. But the essay ends with a delightfully naïve assurance that those who do right and trust in God will surely have their reward.

The other essay is one for which she won a gold medal, made with a clasp and to be worn on a narrow ribbon about the neck. This essay is also most beautifully written without an erasure in it anywhere. It was evidently for a contest in the class in Moral Philosophy. It is full of fervid religious dogmatism. I can see from it that at twenty, at least, Carie had put far from her the pleasure-loving, struggling creature of girlish days and had become a young lady, determined to be noble and Christian. I could almost say, here is a prig in these pages, except that I know well enough that in her there was always that other side of whimsy and humor to save the day. The fact is that to the end of her life if she took up a pen solemnity fell upon her and she put down all sorts of righteous admonitions, which were really admonitions to herself. Even in this little diary she so fortifies herself. I really think the secret of it was the need she constantly conceived to bolster up her own soul. She was continually preaching to herself, fearful lest that laughing heart of hers would lead her astray yet.

Certainly if she had been the person I see here in this essay on *Moral Evidences of Christianity,* this excellent and absurd essay, she could not have so won the universal love of her schoolmates that some of them wrote to her as long as she lived. The girls of her class who were alive twenty-five years after they were graduated made her a beautiful patchwork quilt of silk and velvet bits, and each embroidered her name on her own square and sent it to China to Carie. She gathered it to her breast, smiling, her eyes wet. "Those darling girls," she murmured, although they were all grey-haired women and so was she.

I remember that for once she gave rein to her love of color and she lined the quilt with a gorgeous piece of scarlet brocaded Chinese silk, and it remained to us all a possession and a glory. It was kept in state on the guest room bed, but when Carie lay dying in that Chinese city she called for it and it was spread over her, a covering of love and homage. I am glad for one thing, at least, that she died when she did and did not live to see the day of revolution that came, when it fell into the hands of bloodthirsty, despoiling soldiers! It was then cast lots for and fell to such a dark and savage creature as I have never seen before nor since, and he wrapped it about his naked filthy shoulders.

At twenty-two she was finished and she went home to the village, feeling herself completely a young lady. But the years of restriction in the Seminary and the emphasis on religion had deepened her purpose of going as a missionary. Now she broached the matter to her father. He was completely astounded, very angry, and flouted the whole idea. What, a young and handsome woman go to a country where people were heathen and would as soon eat a Christian as not—what, his daughter?—Never!

Carie, astonished beyond measure, for she thought the project would appeal to her father's profound religious views, promptly lost her none too stable temper. She argued with him ardently that he should be willing to give her to the cause, and he, from whom her high temper and stubborn will came, replied with heat and excessive dignity that there was a sensible limit to everything, even to the worship of God. It was not suitable for a young unmarried lady only twenty-two years of age to go as a missionary.

It was the first time Carie had heard such heretical talk from her father and she burst into angry tears and what had been a high resolve now became also an obstinate determination.

During the Christmas holidays of that year the pastor's younger brother came back. He was taller than ever, paler, more remote. In her new and exalted frame of mind he seemed wonderful. Neale Carter and his set were gross and horrible. Then she heard it whispered among the girls of her age that this young man was to be a missionary. Her heart leaped. *Was it the way?*

One day she took opportunity to speak to him, her usual gay ease strangely and suddenly shy. It was after church service, when people were accustomed to linger about the threshold and about the church green. He inclined his head courteously, as shy as she. She said to him, all her soul shining in her golden eyes, "Is it true you want to be a missionary to China?"

She hung on his answer.

"Yes, I feel it my duty," he replied simply. His high white brow was smooth and pure as he stood, hat in hand, his blue eyes serene.

She cried out, ardently, "Oh, I, too, I have wanted to go for *years!*"

For the first time he looked at her with interest. His blue eyes, vague, a little chill, met her dark glowing ones.

"Do you?" he said.

In later years when she was to know him so well those simple words, "I feel it my duty," were to her the key to his nature, the explanation of his every act, the irrefutable argument of his whole life.

He did not forget. He came to call on her formally, and they talked exaltedly of religion and of their mutual purpose. She watched his face as he talked, explaining to her doctrines that she had not had the patience to read out of the dusty books in the church vestry. It seemed as though God meant them to know each other, she thought. There was no rushing of the blood when they were together. They talked so easily and naturally of good things. Her resolve grew more high and pure. The old, world-loving, high-spirited nature receded. When he had gone away she felt cool and tranquil and religious. There was none of the heat and laughter and joking that made her merry and yet half ashamed when Neale courted her.

One day, very soon, too, a letter came to her. It was a proposal of marriage, carefully written, couched in stiff formal phrases. Since they had a common purpose in life, since they were of one mind, it seemed God's will that they be joined. Moreover, his mother was not willing that he go alone without a wife to heathen lands. It was the one stipulation she made—that he find a wife. It was not easy to find one willing to go so far. He had been waiting for the Lord's guidance. It seemed providentially provided.

She read the letter reverently. With a man like this she could be good. Her vivid, forward-leaping imagination pictured the years together, the stern dependence on each other and on God, each helping the other. He was a man not gifted with words. She who was swift and rich in speech could help him there with his sermons. He could supply the profound learning, she the eloquence—invincible combination! She saw a harvest of dark, white-clad heathen being baptized, following them with adoring eyes—a successful life—all the old, stormy, passionate, pleasure-loving nature conquered forever. With Neale Carter her very soul would have been lost and this without saving his. With this other man not only was heaven sure, but she could bring heaven to many another soul. If there was a moment's shadow and a clutch at her heart when she thought of leaving the well-beloved home and land, the next instant she assured herself resolutely that she knew what she wanted. She wanted righteousness above everything. Surely if she sacrificed all—all—God would give her a sign, some day? She seemed to feel the sign very close when she talked with the young missionary.

But she did not answer the letter at once. She went to her father and told him quietly, her exaltation filling her with quietness, that God had provided a way—that she had decided to marry the young man who was going as a missionary and go with him to foreign lands.

Hermanus at this time was a white-haired and extremely choleric old man, straight as a whip and militant as a little general. He seized his walking cane and marched to the door. As luck would have it, it was about three o'clock in the afternoon, the hour when the young missionary was accustomed to call. There he came, walking slowly up the flagged walk with his usual somewhat hesitant step. The little angry man flew out at him and brandished the cane in his face. The young man drew back astonished.

"Sir, I know your intentions!" roared Hermanus in a voice out of all proportion to his inches. "You shall not have my daughter!"

The young missionary had a certain dry sense of humor which appeared at rare intervals. He gazed down on the little man and answered mildly, "Yes, I think I shall, sir," and proceeded on his way.

Carie waited for him at the door and the last vestige of doubt was gone. Hermanus's opposition had worked well for the young man. She accepted him.

Cornelius then undertook to win over their father, and while the brother himself did not wholly approve his sister's decision, he recognized that she was a grown woman and would do as she wished. Moreover, the young man himself was a good man and missionary work was a noble work if one had the desire to do it and the call. But the gist of the matter was that Carie would do as she wanted to do, and it was better to let her have her way with apparent approval at home than to let her go off against their wishes. Very unwillingly, therefore, after repeated conferences, Hermanus gave his consent.

Thereafter every afternoon at three o'clock the young missionary called at the house, talked alone with Carie for one hour in the parlor, where he called her "Miss Carie" to the day they were married, and at four o'clock had tea with the family at which wine and little cakes were served, according to the family custom.

On July 8, 1880, they were married, Carie in a dove-colored traveling dress, since it seemed scarcely fitting to a missionary to put on the fripperies of white satin and orange blossoms.

At the station there was a moment of slight confusion when it was found the young bridegroom had bought only one place on the train.

"You must remember you have a wife now," his older brother remarked reprovingly.

The truth was that greater than the excitement of his wedding day to this young man was the realization of the young missionary that at last his dream was coming true, at last he was about to set out on his life work. "The Work" he called it then and ever after. The last obstacle had been removed, his mother's stipulation that he find a wife. He had a wife. But he never could quite remember it.

If ever two babes set out on a journey, these two were such babes. Both had lived in small quiet neighborhoods, never traveling farther than to school. Now they set forth sublimely and confidently to go halfway around the world, and they knew only that first they went by land and then by sea. Andrew had fifteen hundred dollars in paper notes from the mission board under which he was going, and he carried these folded in the pocket of his double-breasted long coat. They sat up the whole way across the continent, not knowing there were beds to be bought. When they reached San Francisco they did not for several days go to find passage upon a ship. When at last Andrew went to the water's edge he found the "City of Tokio," a rackety, unseaworthy old hulk, was sailing the next day and he engaged a cabin on it and they prepared for this second stage of their journey.

It had not taken Carie three days of married life to see that in the practical affairs of their life she must take the guiding hand. In prayer and preaching Andrew might be powerful but in business he was as trusting and guileless as a child. He believed implicity in human nature, and although he preached its vileness, he could believe evil of no man except of those who differed with him doctrinally. It was Carie then who arranged for the transfer of luggage and possessions to the ship and who went about discovering the necessities of sea travel.

Who knows at the distance of these years, a half century, what was in her heart as she set sail from the American coast that hot summer's day? Certainly I had it from her own lips once that she had a moment of dreadful panic when she realized she was leaving her own land, and she ran down to her cabin that she might not see the ship pulling away and widening the chasm between her and the beloved shore. She felt at that instant a hostility to this saint to whom she had married herself —nay more, a hostility, instantly repressed, to God Himself, who even at this hour of separation would not speak from the high heaven where He lived to tell her by any sign that she had done well.

The waters over which the careening little old steamer was to bear them for the next month remained for Carie to the end of her life an ocean of horror. She found within an hour of leaving the sight of land that she was no sailor. Seasickness took in her a particularly virulent form, not only of nausea but of violent pains in the head and back, increasing rather than bettering as time went on. She was mountain bred and ever a lover of mountains. She could see little beauty in the sea, and that only of a terrible and overwhelming kind. But this, I think, was partly because it remained forever to her a sign of separation from the land, her own land, which she loved more deeply as years were to pass—so great and unconquerable a separation, indeed, was the ocean that in her last years she would never return to her own country, being compelled to die in an alien place rather than risk a sea journey. Once when she staggered, green with sickness, from a ship's gangplank, she turned her brilliant eyes, humorous even then, to us and said, "I want to go to heaven more than ever now that I know the Bible says, 'And there shall be no more sea there!' "

For a bride it was a circumstance peculiarly trying that she must be sick all during her honeymoon. But certainly it was less trying with Andrew as the bridegroom than it might have been with another. He was singularly oblivious to the appearance of women and even to that of his wife. She saw this and could smile, although it was with hurt, too. I remember she said once, many years later, when her beauty of youth was quite gone, "Andrew has never seen how I looked or what I wore. The only time he ever said anything about my looks was once when I was nearly dead after one of the babies came and he thought I could not live and was unusually moved. That time he sat by my bed and said in the shyest way, 'I never knew before what pretty brown eyes you have, Carie.' That was when I had been married to him eighteen years and had just borne my seventh child! You see what it is to be married to a saint." Then, with that swift, whimsical turning that was habitual to her she added, "Well, I'd rather be married to a saint that never saw my good looks than to a sinner who saw every other woman's!"

In Japan they were both astonished by the civilization and culture evident there even in the brief stops they made in ports. To Carie especially, who saw with delight the dainty miniature beauty of these people, it seemed incredible that so fairy and perfect a nation could be wicked. But Andrew was not thus easily confused by beauty, and was reassured when he saw temples everywhere and people worshipping. Evidently it was a "heathen" country still.

The old "City of Tokio" went no farther than Japan, and they had to change to a sidewheeler that plied the China seas. On this they had an outrageously rough five days' voyage. Before passing into these notoriously wild waters, however, there were two perfect days in the Inland Sea of Japan. There the waters of the ocean are held secure in the islands and mountains of Japan, and tamed and placid, they lie content in their beauty. To Carie this sea remained forever a memory of peaceful loveliness, and she took fresh joy in it on every sea crossing she was to make thereafter.

As they approached China she looked eagerly for the picturesque craggy shores which make the entrance to Japan so memorable, but there was no such shore to be seen. The Yangtse River flowed out solid and sullen into the sea, and its yellow, muddy waters maintained themselves uncompromisingly against the clear sea water. It seemed as though the very ship faltered and stumbled as it crossed the line where the two waters met without mingling. On either side of the ship, as land came into sight, were long, low mud flats. Her heart sank a little. Was her life to be spent in a country without beauty?

Thus they reached China and they disembarked at Shanghai, then as now the chief port on the China coast. They were met on the docks by a contingent of old missionaries, and Carie scrutinized them eagerly to see what manner of men and women they were. She was secretly a little disappointed to find that they differed outwardly in no special way from others. There were no signs of unusual nobility, no signs, either, of anything that was not good. They were a group of good, plain people, a little out of date as to clothing, such as might be found in her own home town. The women eyed with secret eagerness the details of her traveling costume, and it seemed to her pathetic that their first questions were of America. But they were warm-hearted and friendly and it was good to be met.

To these older missionaries it was new strength to see two young, strong Americans fresh from home. There were only eleven missionaries in all, and there had been none to come for seven years. On this first night of the newcomers a dinner of welcome was given at the home of one of the missionaries who lived in Shanghai and there they all went eager to talk and ask questions and enjoy the latest news from home and to give advice.

I can never think of this dinner without remembering Carie as she told of it and of the story that went with it.

After dinner Andrew, replete with good food, and exhausted and drowsy with the sea journey, fell asleep bolt upright in his chair, to the horror and consternation of his young bride, who was across the room and unable to nudge him awake. It was the first time Carie had the experience, although she was soon to find out that it was characteristic of Andrew that all his life when he was weary or bored at any time he could fall gently and obstinately asleep, and awake some time later greatly refreshed and very good-humored. This ability doubtless served him in excellent stead when he was passing through the arduous years of his pioneer work and had an important place in keeping him fit physically, but it never ceased to be an agony to Carie. She learned to sit by him whenever possible, and wake him with a gentle skillful movement, although this had to be done carefully lest he wake with a little audible grunt that drew the attention of all toward him.

One of the times when I saw her most outraged was once when he sat upon a church platform with a group of learned men of whom he was to be one to speak. Finding the speech of the one who preceded him to be somewhat dull, he fell tranquilly and purposely asleep. Carie, well in the front, saw it instantly, and if eyes could have pierced flesh, hers would have pierced him and nailed him to the wall behind. But he slept on and on quietly and she writhed in her seat and all but rose when as he was being introduced he still slept. But miraculously he opened his eyes at the right instant, stared ahead of him and saw the pulpit empty and so rose and began to speak. To the reproaches she never failed to heap on him afterwards he smiled somewhat sheepishly, and to her it was the more exasperating because it was quite true he never failed to wake at the last moment.

The little group of missionaries stayed a week in Shanghai to lay in stores for the winter. This port was the only place in those days where foreign goods could be bought and they purchased even their winter's supply of coal here and shipped it inland on the native junks.

Andrew bought his first British ulster here, for the winters in the Yangtse valley are damp and chill. They bought bedding also and furniture for their room, and Carie bought some rose-colored muslin to make curtains, this somewhat to Andrew's doubt.

Then the little group separated, half of them to go to Soochow, and the others, and among these the new ones, to go to Hangchow. They set sail in slow, heavy old wooden junks and it took them seven days to make the journey from Shanghai to Hangchow, a fact incredible in these days when a good train service brings these cities within half a day of each other and business men from Shanghai weekend beside the West Lake in Hangchow. But in those days there were no other white people in Hangchow than this little group, Andrew, Carie and old Mrs. Randolph in one junk and the Stuarts and their three little boys in the other. The junks lay in Soochow Creek and there they boarded them, and the boatmen poled them through the Chinese city, the banks lined with staring, curious people, crowding to see the strange passengers.

Carie, gazing back at the mass of brown faces, was sorely divided in heart. Here were the "heathen," the people for whom she had given up her own country, for whom she had given her life—oh, she would give herself for them—she would spend herself for them! Then she was moved with revulsion. How dreadful they were to look upon, how cruel their narrow eyes, how cold their curiosity! But the junks glided at last out of the darkness of the city where the houses pressed so hard upon the banks of the canals that they seemed to be spilled over the edges and stood even in the water upon their posts.

In the country, the canal ran smooth and still between small quiet fields and Carie drew breath once more. The wideness of the blue sky, the familiar sight of trees, willow trees such as grew on her home ground, of crops standing ripe for harvest—such sights she knew and did not fear.

It was well that Carie's first experience of the new

country was to be the seven long beautiful days drifting between fields of ripe harvest. Beauty could always win her, and here was beauty; if strange, yet beauty. It was the end of September, opening into October, and the sky was cloudless. Never is sunshine more brilliant in the Yangtse valley then at this time when the heavy heat of summer is gone, and the first touch of autumn scarcely does more than rob the air and the sunshine of their dangerous power, leaving all the pleasant warmth. The masses of feathery, waving bamboo, the low green hills, the winding, golden waters of the canal, the fields yellow with the rich and heavy-headed rice, the small brown villages of thatched houses every half mile or so, the drowsy rhythm of the flails beating out the grain upon the threshing floors, the warm sweet autumn air—it was well for Carie's purpose that her first days in China were filled with such things. She sat on the prow of the junk and gazed about her, enthralled, marveling, in her simplicity, that a heathen country could be so fair.

Sometimes they called to the boatman to pull in to the shore and they would get out and walk. The junks could go no faster than a person could walk unless there were winds and the sails up. But these days of early autumn were brilliantly calm and windless and the junks were pulled by a rope tied to a mast and the other end made into a sling and caught over men's shoulders, and the men walked on the shore along a tow path.

As they went through the countryside Carie looked with eager interest into the faces of the people she saw. They were not hard faced and cruel looking as the people had been in the city. They were sunbrowned, kindly farming folk, curious and gaping at the foreigners, it is true, but answering readily to a smile, and of smiles Carie was always free. Fathers, mothers, little children merry as brown crickets in the earth, she saw them as families and as people earning their living from the soil, and they became human to her, and forever afterwards, I think, ceased to be "heathen." This was to be the keynote of her life among them later, though she had, it is true, a certain amount of race prejudice which was perhaps the effect of the times in which she grew up. But suffering or need or charm of individuals made her quite unconsciously forget her prejudices and she saw people as persons.

I remember a story she used to tell us of her childhood, when although her father would not own slaves, he would not, either, allow his children to play with colored children. At the far end of one of the fields was a tenant house on which a free negro worked for the place. He had a large family of children and Hermanus had a high board fence put up, on the other side of which they must remain. Carie said, "We used to play down in that field sometimes, but I never could enjoy it. Those little colored children would climb up and watch us and look so wistfully at us. One day Luther shouted out, 'We can't play with you!' And the little colored children cried out in a scattered chorus, 'We knows it—we knows we's little niggahs!' I've never forgotten how sad it made me feel, and just for that moment I knew how it would be to be black in a white community. I remember I scolded Luther mightily for being so cruel as to remind them." Her eyes, when she told us, were tender and tragic with the memory. She longed so much for people to be happy.

How many times I have seen her, passing on foot through a little Chinese village, halt, as Christ halted once above Jerusalem to cry out that great, sad cry of his life, "Oh, Jerusalem, Jerusalem!" So I have heard her cry passionately, beholding the oppression of life upon people, "It doesn't need to be so very different from this," she would say. "So little needs really to be changed in these villages—the houses, the streets, the fields, they are all good enough in themselves. I want them kept as they are. But oh, if only the people would not kill their girl babies and keep their women ignorant and bound of foot and if they would not worship blindly through fear only—if only the filth could be cleared from the streets and the half-dead dogs killed, even—it's a beautiful country if only they would use what they have!"

And again she cried, "I don't want them to take anything of ours. If only they would live in their little villages and in their towns and cities just as they are, only make them clean and be good—how beautiful it would all be!"

Never in all her long life among them did I ever see her teach them anything beyond the simplicities of righteousness and cleanliness. It delighted her practical sense to take a native product and show them how to use it well. "You don't need foreign things and lots of money," she would say to a woman. "You have enough of everything if you will learn to use it well." Again and again she would murmur, passing through town and countryside, "They have everything and enough of all except two things, cleanliness and righteousness." These were the two rocks upon which her own life was built.

Passing then, in this first period of her new life, along the fair countryside, her heart was filled with the desire to give them what she had of these two essentials of life. That she found the country lovely to see and the people kindly warmed her very soul and moved her to fresh zeal. In a country so fair as this surely it would not be hard to tell them about the good God. She began those years with a tremendous enthusiasm for life, the life she had chosen. There were so many things she could do—babies with sore eyes, women who could not read—oh, a score of things to do. In the business of the things to be done she almost forgot her secret trouble—that God never had really given her a sign.

They reached Hangchow on a Saturday morning and they walked through the close and crowded streets until they reached the mission compound. Wheelbarrows, sedan chairs, vendors with their baskets slung on a pole over their shoulders, magicians and street fakirs, wayside shops, women washing clothes at wells and shouting amiably the neighborhood gossip, little naked children dashing expertly in and out of the crowded vehicles and legs—it seemed incredible that there could be ways so narrow and people so multitudinous. But from the congestion they stepped into a narrow gateway and all was peace. Here on a green lawn were set two whitewashed mission houses, square and cheap in construction, it is true, but clean and with plenty of windows and long verandas. There was a little whitewashed chapel, also, opening with its own gates into the street. Here was to be their home, here in this mission compound.

In the first house nearest the street was the room assigned to Carie and Andrew and on that very day they settled their belongings and Carie made and hung the rose-colored curtains. They were a comfort and joy to her for many a day.

The next morning, it being Sunday, they all went to church, and Carie and Andrew had an undoubted excitement in this first experience of worshipping their God in a land where He was not known. At the threshold they had to separate, Andrew to go to the men's section, and Carie to go with the other two American women to the women's section. A very high board wall was between the two. Carie sat down and watched while the other two white women spoke to this one and that one of the assembled dark-skinned women. Warm greetings sprang up on every side and Mrs. Stuart chatted easily with them. Carie was for an instant envious, feeling herself tongue-tied because she could not talk. But Mrs. Stuart turned to her, saying, "They are all asking about you. They are so glad you have dark eyes and hair."

Carie smiled; too, then, and felt warm and friendly, and looked with greatest interest at these Chinese women of all ages, most of them with babies in their arms. She looked at their neat cotton coats and wide sleeves and their wide pleated skirts, and saw with horror their tiny pointed feet. That she must change, she decided, with boundless faith in her resources and purpose. Each woman carried a hymn book and a few other books neatly tied up in a blue cotton kerchief. As the service began, Mrs. Stuart went to the baby organ, and immediately there was a great rustling of hymnal leaves. Most of the women were being taught to read, Carie found out afterwards, and they felt their honor depended on their ability to find the hymns as they were given out. Their pastor, who was Dr. Stuart, waited patiently, with a subdued twinkle in his eyes, until with agitated peerings at each other's books and much whispering each had found the place. Then he gave a sign and Mrs. Stuart began to pump the somewhat obdurate and certainly overworked little organ.

No one had thought to prepare Carie for this hymn singing. In the little white church of her childhood the singing of psalms and hymns had been a dignified and beautiful part of the service. She had expected the familiar tunes here, and waited expectantly while Mrs. Stuart played over once, "There Is A Fountain Filled With Blood." The face of every Chinese woman at this point became tense and excited. The instant Mrs. Stuart opened her mouth to sing the race began. Everyone sang as quickly and as loudly as she could, and from the roar that came over the board wall, evidently the same thing was happening on the men's side. Such a mighty noise filled the little chapel that it seemed the roof was like to burst off.

No one sang the tune, but only his own. Carie listened in a panic of astonished mirth. The old lady next to her rocked back and forth squeaking in a high falsetto, gabbling at a terrific speed, her long fingernail following the characters down the page. She finished ahead of all the other singers, slapped her book shut, and sat down in triumph, to tie it back into the kerchief. Envy was writ on the face of the others who saw her and they redoubled their efforts. Meanwhile, the old lady sat composed and enveloped in an air of victory.

It was too much for Carie. She held her handkerchief to her lips and went outside. There safely out of hearing behind the chapel she laughed until she cried. When quiet reigned once more, after the prolonged and lonely voices of one or two of the slowest ones had meandered on in determination to the very end, she went back, glancing at Mrs. Stuart to see how she had borne it. But this was an old story to her. She had closed her book and sat pre-pared for the sermon.

The next morning Carie and Andrew settled to their first lesson in the Chinese language. Their teacher was a very small, dried, wizened, little old man, dressed in a somewhat soiled black robe that flapped about his heels, and he was notable for a vacuous and wandering right eye. His one English word was "yes," but he did not know its meaning and they soon learned it was a habit and not a vocabulary with him.

They had a small lesson sheet with the sounds of the Hangchow dialect plotted upon it, prepared by some American, and a copy of the New Testament in Chinese. These were their textbooks. But the teacher began and by noon they had learned several sentences. Thereafter from eight until twelve and from two to five they studied with the old man, and at night reviewed together what they had learned during the day.

Carie showed at once an amazing facility at the spoken language—a facility which I have been told Andrew found at times a little trying, and which made him some-what stiff, reared as he had been in the doctrine of male superiority. But he was more patient at learning charac-ters than she, and this consoled him, for he considered it the real test of scholarship. Carie's quick ear and re-markably natural pronunciation remained assets to her. Andrew was a little shy at practising what he knew lest he seem ridiculous in his mistakes, but Carie had no such pride or self-consciousness. She used every word she learned on anybody who would talk with her—on the old gateman who was always ready for a laugh, on the cook, on the maidservant in the house. When she made a mistake she could laugh as heartily as anyone and with as keen an enjoyment. She was far too fun-loving for dignity, and with her quick smile and bright dark eyes soon became a great favorite with the Chinese ladies. This was also because there was about her such a warm humanity that none could fail to recognize it. When she saw that these people were like herself, she began to treat them exactly as she would those of her own race, with no sense of strangeness, and this was from no studied effort but only from the natural outpouring of her warmth of human sympathy. Filth and dishonesty were the only two qualities which moved her to indignation and to wonder, fleeting enough, whether they—the people—could be "made good," since these two faults seemed sometimes depressingly universal.

After the day's studying she and Andrew took long walks and they explored the city and countryside. It did not take them long to choose the countryside, for the narrow, winding streets, the beggars, the crowded, unsanitary life, oppressed Carie unbearably. Moreover, crowds followed them thickly wherever they went in the streets and this was unpleasant. But I think she minded most the sad sights to be seen, and perhaps particularly the blind. I have seen her many times stand aside to let a blind person pass, tears in her eyes, a passion of pity flooding her. Man, woman or child, a blind person sent her fumbling in her pocket for money, if the person were at all poor. "Oh, the hopelessness of it!" she would whisper. "So many of them—never to see the sky, never to see the earth—never to *see!*"

But one of their favorite walks was on top of the great city wall, whose ramparts look down over the city and over the West Lake and over the rivers that wind and meet about the city. Here and there were space and air and miles of country to look over and few to molest them. But even here she learned not to look over the wall too closely, for at its foot there were often little dead bodies of children, bodies of those who had died or been killed.

She early came to see the land of China for what it was and is to this day—a great country of contradictions, where the most beautiful in nature and conceived in the imagination of man is inextricably mingled with the saddest to be seen on earth. This compound of beauty and sorrow was to bind her to this land of her adoption most strangely at times, but sometimes it sent her to her room in a terror of repulsion and longing for her home and for her own country.

This saint of Carie's she soon found was very man, too. Before she had been in Hangchow three months she was with child. Children had scarcely been in her scheme, and in her innocence—fatal innocence of her generation! —she did not know what was wrong with her. She dosed herself with numerous liver pills and with quinine and in the end it took the experienced eyes of Mrs. Stuart to suggest the root of the difficulty. When the truth dawned in Carie's mind she received it with mingled feelings and a good deal of surprise. Somehow she had taken it for granted that she would not have children since she had dedicated her life to a cause. Nevertheless, after a short time of reflection and adjustment, she was too much woman not to rejoice and she assured herself that there was no great change in her purpose—it was only a new means of working out that purpose, through home and little children rather than through following after Andrew where he went.

She kept persistently on with her study of the language therefore, although she was very ill sometimes and had to lie down a good deal. It was natural to a person of her buoyant temper that there were periods of reaction and depression, and during these she wondered with something like fear how she could rear children in an environment so different from her own childhood; how keep them to the standards of her race and creed, how protect them from sadness and sights of death. Then homesickness flooded over her with the sickness of her body, homesickness for her own country, for the people she knew in her little home town, people direct of gaze and upright in dealing; for all the clean simplicities of their life.

There was no doctor in Hangchow so when the hour drew near for birth she and Andrew went to Shanghai once more, and there her first son was born, and when he lay in her arms she forgot all her pains of body and mind and again there was joy for a man born. He was a large fair boy with blue eyes and pale gold hair, and her love rushed out to him, and all the deep maternity in her awoke, never to sleep again. It must be confessed that during these years of her child-bearing the impulse of her impetuous nature went out to her children and the home she could make for them and for that time at least her enthusiasm for her cause was in abeyance, rather, subordinate to the other.

When the child was three months old Andrew was detailed to fill the place of another man in Soochow and this meant tearing up the slight roots they had begun to put into Hangchow and a move, not only to a new city but to a new dialect. But there was one compensation for Carie. She could have her own home instead of one room.

The home was only three rooms above the mission boys' boarding school and one had to climb a narrow, winding, outside stair to reach it. But they had the three rooms to themselves, and from the windows one could look out over the city, its dark tile roofs crowded together at every possible angle, and threaded through with narrow winding canals. Just to one side of the school compound and in full view of her window rose that majestic pagoda, centuries old, which still stands to make visible the glory that was old China. Pagan as Carie knew it to be and pagan as she considered it in her downright opinion, yet the purity of its lines and the nobility of the high crown of bronze and the wild sweet jangling of the small bronze bells upon its upturned corners won her to its beauty. There in the shadow of this old pagoda, above the din of the boys playing in the courts below, her little fair-haired American son grew and sat alone and at last crept about the floors and pulled himself up staggering to stare out of the window.

As he grew out of her arms Carie began to take a share in the school which her husband directed. Her attention was first fixed upon the matter of cleanliness. Her sharp eyes detected signs of discomfort in the long queues

the boys wore from their scalps and she fell upon them
with horrified enthusiasm and rubbed insecticide into the
roots of their hair and washed and scrubbed relentlessly,
regardless of all cries and protests. Then she examined
every boy's bed and clothing and fumigated and made
them all clean and uncomfortable with her scouring.

Andrew, laboring over their everlasting souls, would
not have thought of lice and bedbugs. Carie, engrossed in
the necessity for cleanliness, saw Andrew playing with
some refractory lad, and paused to think remorsefully,
"How much better he is than I! How is it I forget so
about souls?"

And she would send up one of her swift, passing
prayers, "God, help me to remember that souls are more
than bodies."

But the next morning her interest would be caught in
the ordering of rice and vegetables for the kitchen or
there would be a little boy who looked pale and she must
coax him to drink a little milk which his Oriental soul
loathed, or there would be itch on another's hands and
she must run for the sulphur mixture. Souls were more
important, that one believed heartily, but bodies were
somehow so immediate.

Her eagerness to be of help at this time led her into
studying medicine out of various books she could buy in
Shanghai, and part of her work each day came to be the
holding of a little clinic where she treated simple diseases
and dressed ulcers and skin infections and gave advice to
mothers about their sick babies. She learned to lance
hideous carbuncles and to treat rotten and gangrenous
bound feet. If her flesh crawled as it often did so that
she could not eat for sickness at times, her sense of humor
saved her. She never failed to smile at the suspicion of
the women over a pill of quinine—how could so small a
thing work any healing for so dread a disease as prolonged chills and fever and turning yellow and fading
away? Without a word but with a twinkle in her eye she
learned to melt the pill in a great bowl of hot water and
hand the brimming, bitter dose to an old lady, who tasting

its extreme nastiness and seeing its vast amount was comforted and drank it down with every assurance of full recovery.

But chief compensation for crawling of the sensitive flesh and the horror at long neglected troubles was the joy of seeing good sound skin grown again and health returning to pale emaciated bodies. This was good. This was triumph.

In this year her brother Cornelius sent her an organ, a Mason and Hamlin organ of good size, such as had stood in the sitting room at home. It had an extraordinarily sweet tone, for Cornelius had chosen it himself with great care and his true ear knew the best. It was six months on the way, having been freighted through the Mediterranean. It arrived on a Saturday evening and Carie could not eat or rest until the box was opened and she and Andrew together lifted out the precious instrument. There it stood, her own! Her very heart was moved and she sat down at it reverently and played one of the choruses they used to sing together at home, "I Know That My Redeemer Liveth," and soon her big, glorious voice was lifted joyously and rang out over the courts and the streets and people stood still in the twilit streets to hear what they had never heard before. Then she sang a hymn in the Chinese tongue and the manservant came and stood in the shadow of the half-opened door and she marked his listening face and it came to her with a great rush of joy that perhaps here was her special gift of service.

Thereafter the organ became as a living person in her life and to this day there are those who think of her always as she looked when she sat there at it, sometimes with her apron on and just as she happened to be in the midst of work and household duties, but always her strong hands gathering great chords of melodies to scatter out and her lovely voice ringing forth. Through all the wanderings she was destined to have her organ went with her, and when her home was a thatched mud hut, the organ stood on a board platform to keep it from the dampness of the earthen floor, but it stood there where she could run to it half a dozen times a day and make it speak.

By the second summer she was again with child and this summer they spent in Shanghai to be near a doctor, for all had not gone well with her. Just as they were about to return Andrew took a severe sunstroke and thus the return was delayed. Carie set herself to tend him then, for the doctor said his life depended on nursing. Edwin, the little boy, she sent with a friend and she gave herself wholly and resolutely to saving her husband's life.

For six weeks he hung on the edge of death and for six weeks Carie did not undress for sleep, but only bathed and freshened herself in the morning and evening and sat beside him and tended him. The doctor marvelled at her vitality. Through the hot, humid days of late summer and early autumn she kept herself fresh in white gowns, a ribbon at her throat, her bright hair waved and immaculate, her heart calm and resolute. She was quite determined that Andrew should not die in the beginning of his chosen career. There was the unborn child to think of, too. For that one's sake she must not let herself be fearful and anxious. Much of the time Andrew was delirious and she had a manservant to help her hold him and she bathed him with cool water until he grew quiet. She was rewarded for he recovered, although ever after he was so muscularly affected in his arms and shoulders that he never got back his suppleness of movement.

With the coming of the cool days of late autumn they were all back in Soochow again and there was born her first little daughter Maude. She was a small, fat, pretty child, very fair of skin, and with brown eyes and curly fair hair. That was a happy winter with the two children. Edwin had grown astonishingly and was beginning to talk and to sing, and Carie delighted to lay the baby in her crib and have Edwin stand at the organ while she played and sang to them. The baby listened, her eyes wide, and Edwin developed a clear, tuneful little voice.

Carie was the gayest mother. She picked up here and

there from her few books and magazines and out of her own head little rhymes and songs and she filled her children's lives with merriment so that later when they looked back and realized with maturity how lonely and narrow an environment was about them, they were conscious of no loss because they had had her rich companionship. Part of this gayety was the overflowing of her own buoyant heart, but part of it was a conscious determination to shield her children from the Oriental life about them, too beautiful as it was, and too sad, for childish hearts. She was always oppressed with the too abundant humanity of the Orient, with its acceptance of human suffering and human passion. She did not want her children to know these too early. Yet what beauty there was that they could bear she wanted them to have. She held her baby up to the window that she might hear the pretty silvery tinkle of the little bells on the pagoda, but she hung a ruffled curtain on the lower sash so that Edwin could not see the beggar who sat all day at the foot, his nose and cheeks eaten away with leprosy.

During that winter she definitely gave her life first to her children and with the deepening experience of motherhood, she began to live more deeply within herself. She began the old pondering about God. All through the years she had looked for a sign from God, a definite sign of approval, and none had come. She could not be sure at any time that the swift emotions of her own heart came from any other source than her own heart and desire. God never came down to her with visible sound or movement. But it seemed to her after a while that her little children taught her much about the God she hoped in— their dependence on her, their little faces turned to catch her mood, their clinging hands—to the end of her life she would say, "How much more they taught me than I ever could teach them!" She would fall into meditation and say at last, "I suppose we understand God's purposes as little as those babies knew mine, even my purposes for them. They trusted me for all their lives, confident in my love, and because of that, willing to believe that I knew best. I think that must be the way we ought to see God—simply trust that He is there and cares."

It came to be her complete creed.

When spring drew near she found to her dismay that she was again with child. It meant that baby Maude must be weaned and this just before the unbearable summer heat came on. But she weaned the child as best she could, without the books and innumerable aids that mothers have in these days.

In spite of every care, however, the change made the child ill, and Carie decided in a panic that they must get to some cooler place if the child was to survive the summer. So she and Andrew and the children set sail for Japan, across the China seas, and on a little Japanese island they spent what remained of the summer. Andrew, absorbed always with his zeal for the Work, traveled about with a Japanese missionary, but Carie spent herself for the children. They lived on the beach all day where the clear sea waves rolled gently up the sands to the fringe of pine trees, and Edwin tumbled in and out of the water and grew brown and hearty, and even little Maude sat with her feet in the warm wavelets and her hands full of sand. She was better but not well, for there was no fresh milk to be had and she could not digest the thick, sweet condensed milk. At the end of the summer she was still frail and thin but alive, and Carie, thankful for this, prepared for the return to China. Andrew was already impatient to be back at his work.

The voyage across the turbulent China seas in the small sidewheel steamer was made yet more rough by the attack of a fierce typhoon. It seemed as though the vessel must founder in the great waves before dawn. Carie was desperately ill and more than a little afraid, but fear and illness were swept up into the greater fear for little Maude, who on the first night out was attacked by a violent stomach disorder that from the very first threatened to be fatal. Carie, racked with nausea, and frightened for the child within her, staggered about in the little cabin of the tossing ship, walking with the sick child. Andrew was helpless except to agonize and pray, for the child would not go to him. The heat was stifling in the close room, and at last Carie, crying that she would rather be swept overboard than endure the gasping of the child, ran out and clinging to the rail, crept up the stairs and to the upper passages. There one of the passengers saw her condition. He was an old missionary, Dr. W. A. P. Martin, and he took the little child gently from her arms and began to walk to and fro with her. It was evident to him at once that the baby was dying and he watched tenderly and sadly as the little face softened and grew unconscious.

There was no doctor on board the little Japanese ship and Carie saw what was to come and was seized with the very despair of death. She flew to the cabin and threw herself upon the floor in an agony of prayer. If ever God were going to speak out of His heaven, let it be now— let it be now! Andrew, praying quietly, could not bear her fevered, importunate besieging of God, and he rebuked her gently, but she turned on him in anger.

"You do not bear these little children," she cried at him. "You do not understand what it is to give your life to the making of a child and then see it die—it's myself dying!" Then she was racked with fury at him. "If it had not been for this other one coming too soon I could have nursed her through the summer and saved her. Oh, Maudie—Maudie!"

She ran back to the passageway upstairs, and there the gentle old man stood still, bracing himself against the rail as the ship flung itself here and there in the winds. He had drawn a corner of the blanket over the baby's face and he stood and waited reverently until the mother came near. Then he went to her and gave her the little, light, still burden. "My child," he said softly, "the little girl has returned to God who gave her."

Speechless Carie took her baby in her arms. It was the first direct blow life had dealt her, and she was helpless against it. She must be alone. She could not bear to see anyone—not Andrew. She went to the end of the passage and opened a small door that led toward the stern of the ship, and slipped out and sat behind a pile of coiled rope. The sea was in great black waves, a leaden, livid light gleaming where a faint dawn shone upon them. Spray broke over her in a mist of foam. She took her skirt and wrapped it about the child, and then she lifted the blanket and looked at the small face. It was white and still and already carven in quiet.

"She really starved to death—she really starved to death—" Carie whispered.

A wave of spray fell over them and Carie covered the child. How she hated this sea—how she hated this sea, the great heaving, insensate thing! Well, at least this precious little body would not be thrown into its vastness to be lost there. She would take it back to Shanghai and lay it in earth where other white people lay.

Over the roaring grey sea hung the grey sky. Where was God in all this? No use praying—no use asking for a sign. She wrapped her arms about the child defiantly and crouched staring over the sea. Then she gave a great sob. Even with all this she must be seasick. Sitting there with her dead baby in her arms sickness overcame her mercilessly, and she must heed it for the sake of life to come.

She rose dizzily and went inside and fumbled for the staircase, and clinging to it with one hand, her baby clasped carefully in the other arm, she crept slowly to the cabin. The wind had blown her long dark hair about her and the spray had wet it. Andrew stood gazing through the thick glass of the porthole, closed fast against the storm. But every instant the dark water covered it as though they were running under the sea.

He turned a quiet face to her. "It is God's will," he said gently.

But she tossed back her wet dark hair and flung out her answer to him, "Don't talk to me about God!"

And suddenly she fell into dreadful weeping.

The crisis of her pain passed at last and she was able

to see it quietly, albeit never without a dreadful hollow aching in her breast. They went back to the house in the shadow of the pagoda, and she set herself steadfastly to her life again, teaching Edwin to read, mothering the schoolboys, teaching them to sing and to learn the history and arithemetic and geography and other subjects of modern importance which distinguished this school from the old classical schools of the country. She made her little house fresh and neat and baked brown loaves of bread and made butter from water buffalo milk which they were able to get now for the first time, and in a hundred ways filled her days full. But she could not bear the tinkling of the pagoda bells and when the wind shook them she rose hastily from whatever she was doing and closed the window. She was thankful when after two months Andrew was suddenly sent back to Hangchow to fill a need there. It was a relief to go back where Maude had never lived and where there were no memories of that short life.

Carie began now to put herself more into Andrew's work. God was not nearer, but she was no longer angry. She was past that now, since anger was so futile. She could even say sometimes, "Thy will be done," without having her heart rise in her throat in hot rebellion. She began to set herself again to the subduing of her passionate, impetuous nature. It was the old struggle. Brooding, she tried to see that this sorrow might be a discipline sent her, there might be a meaning in it. Perhaps God meant to help her and had taken away her child because when she had the little child she was so happy she forgot about God. Perhaps she had to be led by sorrow since she could not be led by joy. She humbled herself to this thought and she began to go often to the little whitewashed chapel that opened off the busy street, and she talked with women there and tried to teach them to read. It was good to have some of them remember her and it warmed her heart to see their friendly faces. When one said, "I have lost my child this year," Carie's eyes brimmed and she seized the brown hand and held it hard in understanding.

But emotionally and physically Carie was too closely knit together. When she was not happy some strength went out of her body and during the winter she grew thin and weary. When spring came and a little girl was born, even this did not waken her to gayety again. It was too soon to have another little girl in her arms. She took the child quietly and lovingly but without joy. The child, whom she named Edith, reflected the mother's heart and was a grave, quiet child, patient for her age always, and even as an infant, responsible and resigned.

In the summer they all went to a mountain top near enough to the city so that Andrew could continue his preaching and teaching but far enough away to get a change of air and to escape the humid heat of the rice fields, stagnant and simmering in the sun. On top of the mountain was a temple and from this they rented two rooms.

It was a new experience for Carie. The deep stillness of the shadowy bamboo groves and the pines, the silent priests stately in their grey robes, the dark cool temple halls with the gods standing dreaming and motionless against the walls—all of this showed her yet a new side of this great, complex country. The huge gods stood in the main halls of the temple, but in the room where she slept with her children a little gilded goddess of mercy looked mildly down from a niche in the wall. Edwin called her "the pretty gold lady," and Carie wove stories for him about the dainty, doll-like figure in its flowing robes, and grew somehow to feel kindly toward this patient little goddess, looking down upon white and alien faces.

When the children lay sleeping and Carie fanned them as they slept, she pondered on the strangeness of her life, she whose room and home had looked out over sweeping meadows and clear country roadsides, over windswept, distant hills and wide skies—she sat here with her two children in a dark room in a Chinese temple, where through the round window she could look down a flagged path to the vast incense urn that stood outlined against the dense green of the bamboos. All through the night and day at long, regular intervals the temple bell reverberated its solitary, resonant note and echoed from the hillsides—a strange, mystic music filled with human sadness.

She was suddenly afraid. She caught her little son into her arms and cried to her heart that she would not have him, a little American boy, shadowed by the strangeness of this land—no, none of her children. Hereafter it would be the first thing in her life to teach them of their own country, that fair, bright America where people believed God was a free spirit and not confined into these fearful and grotesque shapes of painted clay.

Thereafter at dawn and at sunset when the priests chanted their sad chants and little Edwin ran to hide his face in her bosom when he heard the swelling wave of human voices rise into the slow, melancholy music, she comforted him with a voice natural and full of ordinary tones, "That is just their way of singing hymns, darling! Don't you know how we sing, too?"

And putting her cheek against his she would sing softly, "I love to tell the story of Jesus and his love," and from this she would swing into a rollicking nursery rhyme. Soon the temple room was full of her bright ringing voice and the little children were wrapped in the sure comfort of it. To them the sad chanting was only a background, scarcely heard for this warm, glad voice. Always before the end she sang "My country 'tis of thee, Sweet land of liberty." Edwin shouted it with her joyously, the first song he could sing through to the end.

But her body had been subtly broken by sorrow and in spite of her will to do it she could not bring back buoyancy to her step. The languid air was debilitating, and mosquitoes swarmed from the tepid water of the rice fields. No one knew in those days that mosquitoes brought malaria, and Carie took as a matter of course the chills and fevers. Besides this, Edwin caught a dysentery and for weeks was white and weak.

There were other difficulties, too, during the year after the birth of her third child. They were recalled to Soochow, and while they were there the young American missionary doctor, newly come and living in the house with them, was overcome with the extreme sights of suffering and with the immensity of his task, and these preyed upon him mentally until he began to show signs of insanity. Carie with her sharp perceptions had been the first to suspect it, and she lived in tense expectation of disaster.

One day at the end of a meal, when Andrew had already finished and left the house, Dr. Fishe produced a bottle of pills from his pocket and set it before Carie.

"Mrs. Stone," he said persuasively, "you have not been well for a long time. Here is something to make you quite well and at once." He laughed shrilly and strangely, and Carie felt a chill come over her.

"Why, I feel quite well now, Dr. Fishe," she answered in surprise, half rising from her chair.

But he seized her wrist and said in a low, harsh voice, "Swallow them—swallow them all now!"

Carie saw at once she had to do with a madman. Her quick wits did not desert her. She answered quietly, "Just a moment, then, please, until I fill my glass," and taking her empty glass she walked calmly out of the room.

Once outside, she ran for Andrew. He was in the room below preaching to a roomful of listeners from the street, but when she gasped out her story and her fear for the children when the insane man should have found her gone, Andrew went at once. Fortunately, he was the taller and stronger of the two, and after a struggle he succeeded in overpowering the young doctor, whom he found crouched under the table with the carving knife in his hand.

The next day Andrew took the insane man aboard a Chinese junk and watching him day and night escorted him to Shanghai, where he put him in charge of an American who was returning to the United States. The young doctor had periods of complete lucidity when he was well aware of what was happening, and having overheard the American in charge of him explain to some of the passengers that the young doctor was mentally unbalanced and they were not to be disturbed if he acted strangely at times, the young doctor immediately went about informing the passengers slyly that he was taking the other one home because that one was insane. The passengers, and crew remained in doubt for some days as to which was in reality the insane one!

But the incident seemed suddenly too much for Carie, and she found she was tired. Now she noticed what she had not before, that she had a cough and was often feverish. They went to Shanghai to find a doctor, and there she was told she had tuberculosis and must sail at once for America.

She went back to the dingy little room at the mission boarding house to make up her mind what she must do. For one swift glad instant she had thought, "I may honorably go home!" Then she saw Andrew's face, stricken and white. Now in the room she remembered it. He was sitting with his back to her, his shoulders drooping. She said quietly, "Andrew, I'm not going home."

He asked after an instant, "What else can we do?"

She answered passionately, "I won't take you from the Work. I'll never have it said it was I who took you from the Work. We'll go to North China, to Chefoo, and take a house, and you can preach there, and I'll get well by myself."

She watched his shoulders straighten. He turned to her, relief in his eyes and voice. "Well, if you think so, Carie—"

She looked at him at that moment, too proud to speak again, hurt to the soul. Did he understand at all the fight ahead of her? He would accept any sacrifice from her, but it did not matter. She could fight alone. Then it came to her for the first time clearly that there was really nothing between her and this man except these two bonds, the preaching of their religion and the children they had had together, and even the children were but a link of the flesh, for Andrew was not a man who ever understood or loved children. Not that he disliked them, but they did not exist for him in any real sense. His life was wrapped in a mystic union with God and with the souls of men—always their souls. Men and women were first of all souls to him and seldom any more. But to Carie sense was real, life so nearly human flesh and blood entire, and God—where and what was God?

It was the question of her life. If she were to take Andrew away from his work, therefore, what would be left for them together, what tie to bind in any sort of verity? She could not believe that he would ever forgive her, nor, indeed, that he would leave the work he had chosen. She belonged to an age when marriage, at least among respectable and certainly among religious people, was as irrevocable as death. She had pledged herself to a life with him and she would go on with it. She said, therefore, in answer to all suggestions to return to her country, "No, we will go to the northern part of China, and we will see if I cannot grow well there. I shall not give up yet."

But she was fiery independent, when she was hurt, and she would let Andrew draw but half their meager salary, since now for some time she would not be able to do any work in the mission. Then, having said farewell to their little group of friends, they hired a junk and set sail for the coast, and Carie did not know whether ever again she would see these faces, grown familiar with daily association. But she had her pride and her determination to keep her brave.

I remember she said this junk, like many others, was infested with huge rats, and they ran up and down above her head all night on the low hung beams, and one night she was waked out of her sleep suddenly by a great rat struggling in the thick tresses of her long unbound hair. She had to plunge her hand in and seize it and throw it to the floor, and the sleek, writhing body in her hand turned her sick, and she would have cut off her hair if she could for loathing of it.

When they reached the coast they took ship for Chefoo,

a seaport on the coast of a bay in the northern seas off China. But I must not forget to tell that it was on the day before they sailed that she found the oval table standing in the Shanghai second-hand shop, and she was charmed by its slender, firm proportions and bought it then and there from the haggling, bent old man who owned it. This was to Andrew's sore bewilderment, to whom tables were but tables and nothing more, and they had, he thought, already household stuff enough to weary him. If he could, he would have traveled with a scrip and a slender purse and a book, and burdened himself with nothing. But to Carie the beautiful piece of furniture was a thing of delight, and when she was desperately seasick, she fortified herself with the thought of it in all its grace, its fine curves and smooth bright wood, there in the hold of the ship beneath her.

III

ONCE in Chefoo they set about finding a house. Andrew would have rented a place near the Chinese city which stood in the curve below the hills, but Carie would not. She was so ill and weak by now that she knew well it would be a struggle for life itself, and she must have every aid of surroundings. Moreover Edwin still had the dysentery of six months before, and the miserable disease lingered on, and the child was thin and white and scarcely able to stand.

When she told me of this, I saw her eyes grow pitiful and tender. "That poor little boy of mine," she said, "I had to keep him on a starvation diet, and he was so hungry all the time. One day he saw some bits of white on the dining room floor, and he stooped and wet his little forefinger on his tongue and picked them up to eat. He thought they were cracker crumbs and cried when he found they were only bits of lime flaked off the whitewashed wall! It broke my heart."

She longed for him and for herself that she could have

carried them over the sea and land to her own home and into the wide sweet rooms of her girlhood. But since she could not, she found a house set on a hill and above the sea, so that the winds could come in fresh from ocean spaces and untouched by fetid human life. Andrew must just walk a little farther to his work.

The house was a low stone bungalow set on a cliff that ran sheer down into deep, clear blue water and dashing white waves. There was a sandy little garden and a stone wall high enough to keep the children safe but not too high for her to lean upon and pierce the distance with her gaze and dream she saw ten thousand miles away a coastline well beloved.

She set herself then to save her own life. Andrew never saw how truly ill she was, but she well knew that the pain in her side and the constant little dry hacking cough and the feverish languor she had every day held their dire meaning. She had her bed moved to the corner of the porch and lifted and set on bricks so that she might see over the wall to the sea and sky.

To the right of where she lay sandy mountains lifted their gaunt bare shoulders, but of the Chinese city at its foot she could see nothing. It was as she would have it. She must now for her life's sake forget the crowded streets and the blind beggars and the sadness which broke her heart because she could do so little to change it. But lying there she pondered of it still.

Andrew could see the wretched, she thought, and pray for them and be comforted. God would save their souls and in heaven they would be happy. But Carie praying, to be sure, yet prayed with a certain angry passion, for it seemed forever wrong that such things should be and heaven could not wipe out the memory of what had happened on earth. Moreover, if God permitted such suffering, as Andrew said He did for His own wise purpose, still it made no easier the sores upon the quivering flesh and made no lighter the blind eyes and freed no crushed and imprisoned lives. But beyond this she would not let herself go, for there was no answer anywhere. She forced herself, with all the force of the years of training in the village church, to obedience.

"I must just trust and obey," she told herself, chiding her own heart.

But she could not, as Andrew did, withdraw to her room and pray and come out satisfied because she saw only men's souls. No, if her body had broken under her life it was because for the sake of her own anguish she had always to wash and bind and heal where she could and give out medicine to the sick, and where no human could heal and there was none who could remove pain and death she had wept as though it fell upon her own very flesh and blood.

I saw her watch the night through with a mother beside a little dying child, praying aloud as she worked, and at dawn when the child died she seized the little dark dead body and wept in a fury of sorrow and defeat. When Andrew, told of it, opened his eyes in surprise to say gently, "Doubtless it was the Lord's will and the child is safe in heaven," she flew back at him, "Oh, and do you think that fills the mother's heart and arms?" But immediately she said in great dejection, "Oh, I know it's wrong to say that—I know I ought to say God's will be done—but that does not fill empty arms and hearts."

Once I heard someone say of another's dead child, "The body is nothing now, when the soul is gone." But Carie said simply, "Is the body nothing? I loved my children's bodies. I could never bear to see them laid into earth. I made their bodies and cared for them and washed them and clothed them and tended them. They were precious bodies."

Death and sorrow were forever imcomprehensible to her, who was so tender-hearted that she could never hurt any living thing. It was very hard for her to understand the God of the times in which she was reared, and, indeed, she never did.

Out of one of these deep human experiences of hers she had been left with a serving woman who came to her and never left her until old age made her incapable. The woman had been living with a man not her husband who had crushed the skull of her little girl child the morning it was born. Carie, passing the wretched hut on the same day, heard the desperate moaning from within and her quick ear detected more than usual suffering and it was a call to her at once to see what was wrong. She went in and there the little dead thing lay, its brains oozing from the skull, on its mother's knee. The man was lying on the bed of boards, sullen and cursing, and the woman sat dazed. It was a poor little half-starved child at best, and could not have lived long. Carie in her swift vernacular inquired into the matter. The man was thoroughly astonished at her appearance and appalled by her flashing bright eyes and made off without more ado, but Carie turned to the brown woman and knelt down and asked her what had happened, and the two mothers spoke. Carie's hearty, tender anger flew out at the deed and the wickedness of the hand that did it.

"Oh, the poor little thing!" she cried passionately, and the woman staring out over her dead child began suddenly to weep. "Oh, the man ought to be killed!" added Carie fiercely.

"Who can touch a man?" sobbed the Chinese mother. "A man can kill a girl if he wishes—oh, that he had killed me, too."

"At least you will not stay with him," said Carie earnestly.

"Where can I go?" replied the woman. "Men are the same. I have lived here and there, and men are always the same."

Carie felt simple sincerity in the woman, and she said impulsively, "You will come and live with me. I have wanted someone to help me take care of my little girl."

The woman rose slowly.

"I will find a bit of matting to wrap about this little one," she said. "Then I will come."

Never did Carie ask another question of the woman. She received her into her home, taught her the household ways, tried to teach her to read, even, but this the woman could not learn. But through her love for Carie she learned to care most tenderly for Edwin and for the little white baby girl. When she heard of Maude, she wept a little. Then remembering, she said, "Only the Master did not strike her dead with a stone as she suckled at your breast."

"No," said Carie pityingly, in a low voice. She saw an opportunity. "We do not allow such things in our country," she said. "It is because we think our God teaches us to be kind."

Ah, fair country of hers, she thought ardently, dear God, in whom believing men learned to be good!

"I should like to know about that," said the woman. Carie, half halting, began to tell her. After all, was she not taught more by this simple woman than she could teach, she thought? God must be, since where He was not, men could grow so beast-like. By such perceptions, her own hopes grew more strong sometimes.

Thereafter wherever Carie went the woman followed and was a part of the home and nurtured all the children that were yet to come to Carie and Andrew. Years after when these children loved and teased Wang Amah or, as they called her, "Foster Mother," I remember Carie looking lovingly at the old woman, grown lean and wrinkled and white-haired, and once she said, "I believe Wang Amah was what people call not a good woman and I am afraid she will never understand very much of the gospel. But I have never seen her unkind to one of the children, nor have I ever heard her speak an evil word, and if there is no place in heaven for her, she shall have half of mine—if I have one!"

Wang Amah was in Chefoo with them too, and she cared for Carie and the children and made it possible for Carie to lie in bed and be carefree of the children. Andrew went on with his preaching, fervent ever and as oblivious to all else as was Saint Paul. But Carie lay in the keen pure air, sleeping, reading, eating, growing determinedly back to health.

At the end of six months the cough was gone, and she could get up and work lightly for a few hours every day about the house and garden and have no resulting fever. It was one of the happiest times of these years, these months of convalescing in the little house perched high above the sea, with nothing between her and her own land except the straight ocean. She had the satisfaction of seeing Andrew busy in his chosen work, she felt the rush of health again in her blood, and she was saturated with the keen beauty of sky and hills and sea.

Great joy it was to us all when she could begin to sing, at first softly and in time with full tones again.

For the children this illness of Carie's had its good. She spent much time watching them play and wondering over them and taking pride in them. She told them stories and taught them not to imitate some of the things they saw in the life about them. She said often, "We are Americans! We do not behave in that way."

Fourth of July was a gala day always. There was a flag she had made herself, and there were firecrackers and "The Star Spangled Banner" sung about the organ. Long before the children had ever seen America they learned to call furlough time "going home."

At sunset oftentimes they sat upon the beach and looked out over the water and Carie talked to them of the land, their own land, that lay over there and to which they belonged. She talked of the big white house and of the meadows, of the orchard and the fruit they could pick and eat raw, it was so sweet and clean with rain and sun. It sounded like heaven to the little white children who all their lives were accustomed to be watched sharply lest they put something into their mouths which was unsterilized and so fall ill, as Edwin had in some unknown way, in spite of every precaution, so that after months he was only getting back to his usual health. To the end of their days for those children America remains the magic country where water need not be boiled before drinking it, and where apples and pears and peaches may be plucked from a tree and eaten so.

Every day they went sea bathing unless there was a typhoon and the waves too rough and a curious thing happened once which remained a story to tell in after years. Carie's hand was very thin still, and one morning in the water her wedding ring slipped off unnoticed, and only later did she see it was gone.

She went to the beach at once and searched, and they all searched but to no avail. She hired a little Chinese beach boy to dive for it in the spot where she had bathed in the morning, but he found nothing. Late that afternoon in a last effort, although she had quite given up hope, she walked slowly along the beach, and suddenly the last rays of the slanting sun seemed to penetrate the smooth, unruffled water. A ray gleamed to the very bottom, and there in a shallow basin lay the ring, glittering. The little boy dived once more and brought it up, and she placed it in triumph back on her finger. Andrew, told of it, remarked placidly, "I felt you would find it. I prayed."

When she told this tale in after years, her children always clamored, "Was it really because Father prayed, Mother?"

Her bright eyes twinkled, and she said, "Perhaps—but it wouldn't have been seen if I hadn't gone back once more. It is right to pray, of course—but it always pays to try once more yourself, too!"

Now that Carie was well again, she found she must earn money somehow until such time as she was strong enough to leave the seashore and go back into the proper field of Andrew's mission. Summer came, and there was a little group of white people who came to the seashore. Carie moved her own family to the attic rooms and filled her house with the visitors and thus earned enough to pay for what she had forfeited of salary.

But more important to her than the money was this test of her strength. She had to make bread, to wash, to cook, to care for the dozen persons in the house with no other help than a manservant and Wang Amah to help with the children. She was able to do it all, and besides found herself again pregnant. But there was no return of fever or cough and she felt herself cured. At the end of the summer when guests were gone, she closed the quiet little sea-enclosed cottage with its sandy garden, and they returned again to South China.

But she begged Andrew not to go back to the mouth of the Yangtse where they had been. She was well but not strong, so they were sent to a middle region to the river port, Chinkiang, a city on the river and famous from the times of Marco Polo for its great temples and its pagoda and for its rich commerce, standing as it long did at the intersection of the river and of the Grand Canal. Carie loved it immediately for the hills sweeping up from the river. But it was a place too cosmopolitan for the pioneer blood in Andrew's veins. There were other missions and white men there, and he longed for the great spaces where there was not one to preach to the multitudes. He was discontented, and Carie dared not think of a garden until his mission, realizing that he was his best at pioneer work, gave him leave to go where he liked. He hired a house, three rooms above a Chinese shop on the river's edge, and there he left the family and then he took a junk and set sail for the upper reaches of the Grand Canal into the northern parts of the province of Kiangsu.

Once more Carie set herself to the making of a home for the children. The three rooms looked over the Yangtse River, broad and swift and yellow with the earth it had torn away from its banks in the thousands of miles it had come racing from its sources. During the months to come Carie grew to hate and to fear this great implacable river, so swift in its gorges, so sluggish and sullen in its lower spread over the land. It became a symbol to her imagination of the flooding, overpowering, insensate life of the Orient, which seemed to swallow up all other life which came in its way, and against which she braced herself every time she built her American home for her children.

She sat sewing at the window often, and often she lifted her eyes to look out over the slowly swirling, eddying expanse of the river. She saw the ponderous ferries coming back and forth from the city on the other side; she saw the light, skiff-like sampans drifting across like chance leaves dropped from a tree, caught in the cross currents sometimes so that the sampan men had to use the greatest skill in weaving in and out of the net of waters.

In the spring the river rose high, swollen with the snows from the mountains and gorges in its upper parts, and then it was a dreadful and an angry thing. She could scarcely bear to look at it, for more than once she saw boatloads of people overturned and struggling in the water and none saved. Twice she even saw a ferry boat, filled too full with people hanging on the very edges, turn over, heaving like a great beast, and float bottom side up. There was an instant when black heads bobbed in the yellow water and arms flung themselves despairingly upward and then the river pulled them all down and went on as before, except that the boat twisted crazily here and there.

It was said that none who fell into this river could ever be saved, so deep and swift under the smoothly dimpling surface were the cross currents. Every few days a sampan was caught and pulled under. Yet with the curious fatalism of the Orient, the people continued to ply back and forth in every sort of slight craft over the dangerous waters. But Carie grew to hate the river with a deep hatred because she saw how it oppressed people and most of all the people who trusted to it for a living. She had continually to watch Edwin and Edith, lest standing at the window watching the ships as they liked to do, they might see the terror of struggling, sinking men and women.

She had learned by now to make a home where she must, and she made a home here by this river, even while she hated it. The three rooms she whitewashed and she hired a native painter and had him paint the floors and woodwork. Then she bought white muslin stuff at a Chinese cloth shop, such as they use for mosquito nets—the rose curtains were worn out long since—and she made dainty ruffled curtains for the windows, wide enough, too, so that sometimes she might draw them across the cruel river. And because there was no place for a garden she nailed outside the window an empty milk box and one day she took the children and Wang Amah and they went to the hills that bordered the city and brought back healthy black earth to fill the box, and in it she planted geranium slips she had brought back with her from the sandy little garden in Chefoo and the roses she kept with her always. Soon there was a flare of color to look over when she saw the river.

Beneath the three rooms which were all that Andrew could find to rent, there was a compradore's shop, where a Chinese proprietor sold a mixture of foreign tinned food and Chinese produce and especially foreign whiskey and brandy. The few white people in the port traded there and fewer Chinese. The chief patrons were the sailors and soldiers from the American and European warships that harbored at the docks from time to time. The river was so vast and deep that these great ships could penetrate yet much farther than this port. To Carie it was a heart-warming sight to see the American flag waving stoutly above that dark and dangerous river.

Nevertheless, it was these men from her own country whom Carie learned to pity much. They came ashore eagerly, crude young fellows from every state in the Union, laughing, brawny, anxious for fun. There was nothing for them to do, however, and failing else they could crowd into the filthy little compradore shop and buy stale chocolate and English biscuits and above all bottle after bottle of Scotch whiskey. Far into the night and until dawn she would hear them from her room above, singing and shouting and weeping drunkenly. Bottles crashed against the walls and threaded through the din she could hear the high, mosquito-like falsetto of the sing-song girls from Chinese brothels. Sometimes there were screams and cries, but what went on she would not ask, stricken with sorrow for these boys so far from home, and ashamed because they were her countrymen and acted this way before a people alien and already proud and scornful.

Sometimes in the morning after such a night she went down to the shop to buy something and everywhere there would be a wreckage of broken china and merchandise scattered, and the wryfaced, yellow proprietor stood looking at the devastation glumly. Once she asked him, "Why do you sell the stuff to them when it makes them so wicked?"

To this he grinned and answered, "Oh, s'pose white man makee break, I makee him pay!"

But she could not forget her pity and her shame for her countrymen, and so she began to do something she continued for many years. When a foreign ship was due in harbor she baked cakes, great snowy coconut cakes and rich black chocolate cakes whose feathery texture she had learned to make in the cool tiled kitchen at her home, and pies and cookies, and she invited the boys to tea. There was little in common between the raw lads who crowded in, grinning with shyness, to the small rooms, and this woman, cultivated and gracious. But to her there was the deep tie of race and of country, and it warmed her heart to see them stuffing good cake and pie and drinking gallons of lemonade. When they were fed to capacity, she sang to them and sometimes just sat and let them talk to her, woman-starved as they were. When they were gone, she had a triumph in her that for at least one time she had kept them safe—had protected them and given them a little of America.

During this winter a little boy was born, whom she named Arthur. Again it was a blue-eyed, fair-haired child, and again she found fresh joy in this fresh life. No child of hers ever failed to be greeted with a great rush of pleasure, whatever his coming cost, and Wang Amah was overjoyed this time because it was a son. The baby was two months old before his father saw him, a pretty boy, but not too strong from the first.

In Carie's diary, kept intermittently through these years, I find again and again this exclamation, "How rich I am in my children!" Without the friends who would have normally been hers in her natural setting, and with Andrew away on his long journeys, she was nevertheless content with her children and they with her. Once when we were listening to a story a woman was telling of a great romantic love in her life, I saw in Carie's eyes a certain wistful look. But it passed soon, and she said quietly, "My children have been my great romance."

Edwin and Edith both showed signs of unusual mental ability, and it was her delight to satisfy their craving for reading and singing. What was ahead in this strange life of hers she did not know, but this winter of waiting she gave herself freely and wholly to the children. There was no garden where they might play, and the street was vile and crowded, but every fair morning when the day's work was arranged for, she and Wang Amah took the children, Carie carrying the baby, and they walked through the back streets where they would attract least attention to the road which led to the hills. Fortunately, it was not far, and they soon reached a road which wound under trees and bamboos up to the green gravelands.

It never failed to shadow Carie, these acres of graves, green in the spring and summer, and stark and brown in winter when the grass had been cut from them for fuel. She used to ponder on these lives thus buried and often forgotten. Some of them, the small, close-set graves, were those of soldiers who fell in a war; the big ones set about with earthen walls belonged to a wealthy man and his family; each had its meaning. But she always protected the children from such sadness, and they played happily over the graves, plucking wild flowers and running up and down the steep slopes. Later when they went to their own country they were astonished at the smooth graveless hills there, and they realized for the first time that all their days they had played upon the graves of the dead. So did this American mother shield her children and keep them gay.

The hillside where they played most frequently was in the shadow of a fort on its crest, and there was a field where the soldiers marched, and the children loved to watch the red and blue clad soldiers tilting with spears and swords, or to hear the firing of the one old antiquated cannon, embedded deep in the mud of the wall about the fort.

At the foot of the hill the river curled. It was gradually receding, leaving a flat rich plain from which rose abruptly the sharply pointed island called to this day the Golden Island. An exquisite pagoda, upon which Marco Polo gazed in his time, pointed into the air from the curved roofs of the temple on the island.

But if the children loved the flashing soldiers and the sudden spurt of the funny little cannon, the mother loved the distant mountains that rose in peaks along the river's edge. Clear and blue at noon, misted at morning and evening, Carie loved them well and they comforted her somewhat for that other line of mountains, lifted against the American sky, ten thousand miles away, around the plains of her own home.

Summer drew near again, the summer that Carie dreaded every year for its dragging lengths of humid days. The stench from the garbage-filled streets rose into the three little rooms. The geraniums sickened and died in the heat and the roses faded. The flies swarmed from the piles of half-rotting filth, smoking under the burning sun. The hot air hung like a foul mist. Somehow, Carie told herself, somehow she must get her children to the hills.

On one of the hills not far from the fort there was an old mission compound, and there after much inquiry she found a bungalow empty for the summer. It was a low square house with six rooms, three on each side of a hall running the length of the house, and on two sides of the house was a veranda. It was paradise enough after the three rooms above the crowded, noisy street. There she moved, and the summer passed. Sometimes she grew impatient with the centipedes that she hunted every night lest they creep into the children's beds and sting them and make them ill, and the ponds and rice fields in the clustered valleys about the hill bred many mosquitoes, and the great jars of the nightsoil which the farmers used for fertilizing their fields bred clouds of flies. But at least one could look out over fertile valleys and low hills covered with bamboo and the cruel river was a mile away and only lay harmlessly on the edge of the horizon in a broad band of yellow. In the early morning a dense, silvery mist filled the valleys and above it the hilltops rose like green islands. It was beautiful and the more so because it made Carie think of her home, except that these mists were hot and heavy and the mountain mists, in West Virginia were keen as frost at dawn.

But best of all there was a little grassy plot where the children could tumble and a bit of ground for a garden. Carie planted flowers and rose early to cultivate the earth and coax them into speedy blooming before she must leave them. It was the first real garden she had ever had in this country.

But the summer ended and Andrew came back, bearing news of a house ready for them now up the Grand Canal in a city called Tsingkiangpu, which he had made his center of work during all these months. From this place he traveled over a wide radius of country, by muleback, by cart, and on foot, preaching and teaching his message in hamlet and town and city. Now he felt familiar enough in the central city to have his home there and so he had rented and repaired a Chinese house.

Regretfully, for she had loved the square bungalow, and her flowers were still but buds, Carie packed her bags and her furniture and her babies and with Wang Amah they boarded a junk and after ten days of leisurely sailing and towing up the placid canal they reached the old Chinese city, where they were the only white people. Andrew had a house unusually large and with a big court. It was a house said to be haunted by the ghost of a woman, an ill-treated wife of the former owner, who appeared in the form of a weasel, and no one dared to live in it, and so the owner was glad to rent it even to a foreigner.

But whatever the reason, Carie was grateful for the

house, and once more she set herself to making a home. Clean whitewashed walls—she had almost a formula now —wide windows opened in the walls and fresh ruffled curtains, clean matting on the floors, the court planted with grass, flowers again, chrysanthemums bought from flower vendors and gay little single roses of red and pink and yellow. Then when the beloved organ and table were in their places and beds and a few reed chairs and a kitchen made, there was home again. Outside the noisy street ran east and west through the city and was the great thoroughfare for business, and there was the roar of the city, the shouts of hawkers, the cries of chair coolies wending their way through the crowd, the squeak of wheelbarrows. But inside the wall and the gate there was this spot of peace and cleanliness where the American woman built again a little fragment of her own country where she might rear her children and into which she often brought Chinese women who marveled and sighed to see how fair it was.

Andrew had opened many street chapels in the city, and now he had a network of preaching places through the surrounding country and he came and went among these, filled with the zeal of his mission. He had by this time a very good grasp of the language also, and part of his time he spent in making books for his listeners.

Carie at this time of her life did not follow him away from her home and children, but she went often to the chapels and played the baby organ, leading the singing in her clear voice, and after Andrew had preached she taught little groups of women who came to hear what the strange doctrine was about. Most of these women were sad, disappointed creatures, weary of life and borne down by some sorrow, and disgusted with the exactions of the priests in their own religions. Some could not understand the new religion; indeed, it is doubtful if the words Carie spoke ever carried the message she tried to put into them.

Stronger message than her words was the swift and

native sympathy of her nature when she listened to their sad stories. Her instant impulse was always "to do something about it." They learned to call her "The American of Good Works," and many women came to her at her home, women whom she had never seen but who had heard of her, and when their stories were told the end was always wistfully said, "They tell me you always can do something—that you always think of a way."

This was her great service, that she was always ready to stop and listen to their sorrows. I remember her sitting, many a day, at the window of her little living room, her mobile face twisted with sympathy, listening earnestly to a broken voice that went on and on. The children played and shouted happily in the garden, and every now and again she would look at them and smile, but she listened still, her eyes sad. Many of these women were among the most downtrodden of their kind and had never in all their lives had the comfort of having one sit down to hear the burden of their poor hearts, and it seemed they must tell her over again and again for the relief it gave to speak to a listening ear. Once I heard a woman say to her, "Tell me what to do and I will do it. Tell me what to believe and I will believe. There has never been one in all my life long who cared to heed one word I might say or one tear that fell from my eyes. My father did not love me for I was a girl; my husband did not care for me; my son despises me. I have been despised all my life because I am a woman, ignorant and ugly. Yet you, an American and a stranger, pay heed to me. Therefore what you believe I will believe, for it must be true to make you like this—kind, even to me!"

It was one of the happiest winters in these years of her life. The little Chinese house was cozy with a tin stove made according to directions at the tinsmith's shop, and flowers bloomed in her windows. She had a gift for flowers and they always bloomed for her easily, and her rooms, which would otherwise have been bare with only the scanty furniture she had, seemed always hospitable and furnished because of the growing things.

But the spring and then the summer drew near again. If only there need be no summers, Carie thought! This year was worse, for it was a summer of unprecedented droughts. Day after day through the spring no rains fell, and farmers, waiting for the floods of the rainy season to fill their rice fields, saw their young crops dry up before their eyes. Midsummer came on, hot beyond belief. There was no hope of rice harvest then for this year, and in haste the country people planted a little corn here and there so that they would not be entirely destitute.

Carie, with her sharp perceptions ever sensitive to changes in the moods of people, felt such a change in the temper of the people in the city. Few came to Andrew's little chapel. There was a noticeable lessening of the crowds that had come at first—one Sunday there was not one person. The next day Wang Amah came back from her marketing and said to Carie, "It is better for you not to go out now on the street." When pressed she added unwillingly, "The people say the gods are angry because foreigners have come into the city. There has never been a drought like this before, and this is the first year there have been foreigners in the city to live. The gods are angry, therefore, they say."

Even Andrew, usually oblivious to all save the Work, noticed a hostility of scowling faces when he spoke in the streets or when he tried to give away his tracts. Once or twice a man took a tract and tore it up before his face. It was a significant act in a country where the printed character is sacred for its own sake. But Andrew was of a nature made more steadfast by opposition, and when for the time he found his work obstructed in the city he went on one of his long country trips, to be absent for many weeks, and Carie was left alone with the children and Wang Amah.

One hot August day she sat by the window sewing. The air was heavy and oppressive, and every sound from the street seemed magnified through its density. She heard a whisper of voices beneath the open window. She listened, her ears sharp with apprehension. Two men were plotting something.

"Tonight at midnight," they said, "tonight at midnight we will force the gates and kill them and throw their bodies before the gods so that rain may come."

She rose quickly and went to find Wang Amah. "Go out and listen about the streets," she said. "Find out if you can what is being planned for this night." And then she whispered what she had heard.

Without a word Wang Amah put on her poorest coat and went out. In a little while she came back, her eyes staring. She shut all the doors carefully and then went near to Carie and put her lips to Carie's ear.

"Oh, my mistress," she panted, "they are coming to kill you tonight—you and the children. Every white person is to be killed."

Carie looked at her. "Do you think they will really do it?"

"Why not?" answered Wang Amah, heavily. She took up the corner of her apron and wiped her eyes quietly. "All these people you have been kind to—" she muttered, "all these people—not one of them will dare to help you now. If they came forward they too would be killed." Carie stood still, saying nothing, thinking fast. Wang Amah looked into the white woman's eyes. "But there is still I," she said firmly.

Carie went to her and took her hard, faithful brown hands. "I am not afraid," she said quietly. "I will go and pray to my God."

She went into her room then and shut the door and fell upon her knees by the bed. For a moment she was dizzy with the panting of her heart. Would this day really bring the end to her life—to the children's short lives? She sent her heart upward into that vague height where she had been taught God dwelled, and she prayed, "If it is Thy will, save us, but in any case, help me not to be afraid." Then after a long pause she prayed again. "If the time comes to die, help me to have the children go first."

She knelt for a long time then, thinking of what she must do. Then again for a long time she was silent, waiting. No answer came, as none ever had, but at last she rose, fortified with her own courage and a good stout anger that came welling up.

"I shan't let myself be killed by a lot of superstitious, ignorant people, and I can't have the children killed," she determined, somewhat amazed at her own calmness. Well, she would just trust in God, silent as He was, and not fear what men could do to her.

That night she put the children to bed early and then sat quietly sewing. All day her anger had stayed by her. "I, have no notion of dying," she said aloud to herself with great firmness. Gradually it had come to her what she must do.

She moved to the window and as she sewed she listened. The murmur of the city drummed through the stifling, dusty air. She listened to it, strung tense to catch a change in its tempo. About midnight the change came. The murmur rose and seemed to eddy about the walls of the house. The hour was coming. She rose and called softly to Wang Amah who sat silent in the shadow of the court, "Wang Amah, please prepare the tea now."

Then she went downstairs and set out cups and plates upon the oval table and placed cakes on plates. Then when all was ready as though for a feast she swept and made the room spotlessly neat and set the chairs as for guests. Then she went to the court and to the front gate and threw it wide open.

On the threshold stood a vanguard of men, their faces invisible in the darkness of the hot night. They drew back into the blackness but she did not seem to see them, nor did she falter. She went back to the house and left the door open into the court, turned the oil lamp high, so that the light streamed outside, and then went upstairs and roused the three children and dressed them and brought them downstairs. They were astonished and silent with the strangeness of the proceeding, but she talked to them naturally, sang a little song to them, and sat them on the matting of the floor and gave them their Sunday toys to play with and they fell to playing happily. Then she took up her sewing again and sat down. Wang Amah had brought in pots of tea, and she stood behind the children, motionless, her face expressionless.

All about the house the murmur increased until it was a roar of many voices. When the voices became articulate and very near Carie rose casually and went to the door and called out, "Will you come in, please?"

They were already in the court then and at the sound of her voice they swelled forward, a mass of sullen, angry men of the lower working class, in their hands sticks and clubs and knives. She called again kindly, her voice made bright by sheer will, "Come in, friends, neighbors! I have tea prepared."

The men paused at this uncertainly. A few pressed forward. Carie poured the tea busily and came forward bearing a cup in both her hands as the polite custom was. She presented it to the tall, surly, half-naked man who seemed to be the leader. His mouth gaped in amazement but he took the cup helplessly. Carie smiled her most brilliant smile upon the faces that gleamed in the light from the wide flung door.

"Will you come in and drink tea for yourselves?" she said. "And sit down also. I am sorry my humble house has not enough seats, but you are welcome to what I have."

Then she stepped back to the table and pretended to busy herself there. The children stopped playing, and Edwin ran to her side. But she reassured them gently, "Nothing to be afraid of, darlings. Just some people come to see what we look like—such funny people, who want to see what Americans look like! They haven't seen Americans before."

The crowd began to edge into the room, staring, gaping, momentarily diverted. Someone whispered, "Strange she is not afraid!"

Carie caught the whisper. "Why should I fear my neighbors?" she asked in well-simulated surprise.

Others began to examine the furniture, the curtains, the organ. One touched a note, and Carie showed him how to make the sound come. Then she slipped into the seat and began to play softly and to sing, in Chinese, "Jesus, Thy Name I Love."

Dead silence filled the room until she finished. At last the men looked at each other hesitatingly. One muttered, "There is nothing here—only this woman and these children—"

"I go home," said another simply and went out.

Others, still sullen, lingered, and the leader halted to look at the children. He held out his hand to Arthur and the rosy, friendly little boy, having seen brown faces about him all his life, smiled and seized the man's lean dark forefinger. The man laughed delightedly and cried out, "Here is a good one to play!"

The crowd gathered about the children then, watched them, began to grow voluble in their comments, picked up the American toys to examine and play with them. Carie, watching, was in an agony of fear lest a rough movement might frighten one of the children and so change the temper of the men. Wang Amah's dark face was sternly watchful at the door. At last the leader rose and announced loudly, "There is nothing more to do here. I go home."

It was the signal to follow. One by one, with backward stares, they passed into the court and into the street. Carie sat down again, suddenly faint, and taking the baby into her lap rocked him gently. The men, lingering at the threshold of the gate, looked last upon her thus.

When they were all gone Wang Amah crept forward and seized the baby and held him to her fiercely.

"If one had hurt him I should have killed that devil," she whispered, and from the bosom of her coat Carie saw the handle of the carving knife protruding. But Carie only laughed tremulously now, and lifting Edith in her arms and taking Edwin by the hand she led the way upstairs. She bathed the children again in cool water and put them back to bed.

Then she went down and closed the gate of the court upon the street, now silent and empty with the night before dawn. At the door of the house she paused. A wind had risen out of the southeast, a wind like the herald of a typhoon. She listened; it rose suddenly and blew in a gust through the open windows and the curtains streamed out straight. It was fresh and cool with the coolness of the distant sea.

She went upstairs to bed then and lay still, listening. Would the wind bring rain? She lay sleepless for a long hour and fell at last into light sleep, and later awoke. Upon the tile roof above her was the music of rain pouring down, streaming from the corners of the house, splashing upon the stones of the court. She lay transfixed with joy, her body relaxed at last in the cool damp air. The dreadful night—the dreadful night was over!

She rose and went to the window. Grey day was beginning over the housetops, but not a soul stirred. Exhausted with the past heat, the city slept and into the empty streets the good rain poured in long steady lines. They were saved. . . . Was it a sign at last?

The end of the summer drew near and Carie was joyous with relief. Then as though joy was never to be lasting for her, one day in early September Arthur fell ill with a sudden fever. The child had had a bad fall the day before into a tiled drain in the court and had seemed languid for some hours after it, and Carie had watched him anxiously. But by evening he had seemed his usual gay self.

The next morning, however, the languor had returned, and by noon he was flushed with fever and she dosed him with the simple remedies she had and bathed him in cool water and Wang Amah fanned him without ceasing. Still the fever mounted and by night the child was unconscious. All afternoon he had been moaning in pain, but he was too little to tell where the pain was, although

Carie examined his little body again and again. At last when he fell into a dreadful, white-lipped stillness she hung over him in terror and helplessness. Wang Amah felt his little feet.

"He is dying," she said gently.

There was no white doctor in the city, but the mother could not let the child die without anyone. Frantically she turned to Wang Amah. "Go—go—find the best Chinese doctor in the city—ask him to come at once—tell him a son dies!"

Wang Amah disappeared instantly and in a short time came back with the doctor, a small, scrawny old man in a dirty black robe and wearing on his nose huge brass-rimmed spectacles. He entered the room silently and imperturbably without looking to right or left, and went straight to the little bed. He thrust out an unwashed and long-nailed hand like a claw from his sleeve and delicately he held the tiny hot wrist between his thumb and forefinger. Thus he sat for a long time, his eyes closed. Then he rose, and drawing a bit of folded paper from his bosom and his ink and brush from his girdle, he rapidly brushed a few hieroglyphics.

"Take this to the medicine shop," he directed Wang Amah. "Bring it home and brew it in hot water and give the child a quart to drink every two hours." He held out his hand for his fee and was gone.

Wang Amah went with the bit of paper and brought back a bundle of herbs and a large brass ring covered with verdigris and green with age. She hurriedly prepared to make the brew, but Carie called her, "Amah—Amah!" The cry was a scream and Wang Amah ran to the sick-room. "My baby—my baby—"

Carie had him in her arms. He was dying in a convulsion. Wang Amah gave a grunt of comprehension and seized from the bed a little garment he had worn and ran out, grasping a lighted lamp as she ran. A moment afterwards Carie heard her voice floating upward from the street.

"Child, come home—come home—"

Over and over the call came, fainter and fainter in the distance.

It was a cry Carie had heard many times and many times had shuddered at its sadness. Many a time, too, she had passed a weeping mother carrying a lighted lantern and in her hand a little coat, and Carie's heart had grown heavy with sympathy, for she knew that somewhere a little child lay dying and the mother in her last hope had gone forth to call home again the small wandering soul.

Now the little wandering soul was the soul of her own child. She held the frail body to her and as she held him he shivered and was still.

The next day she sent out a runner to find Andrew wherever he might be, for there was no other post service in those days. Wang Amah bought a little coffin and Carie lined it with a bit of blue silk she had and together the two women bathed the fair little American child and laid him in his place, and from their grievous weeping no one could have said which was the mother. The coffin-sealers were sent for, because the air was still warm with summer. Then when all was done Carie sat down and waited for her husband's coming, and he came the next night, weary and exhausted with forced travel. Carie met him dry-eyed now and desperate.

"I must go away," she said to him. "I must see a white woman—someone of my own kind. Let us take him and put him beside the other one in Shanghai. I can't have— my baby—lying alone here in this—this heathen city."

Andrew recognized the despair in her voice and assented. The very next morning they hired a junk and set out for the coast, a journey of fourteen days by canal and river.

But no one had told them that in Shanghai cholera was raging. There were no newspapers, no post offices to carry letters quickly. They reached the dingy mission boarding house through streets dark with death. The first day Carie counted more than fifty coffins pass by the window. She was terrified, and they made haste after the funeral to go away again.

But at dawn of the day they were to return Carie was seized with violent vomiting and purging, and an hour after Edith, then nearly four years old, was taken also. Andrew tried to find a doctor, but none could be found, for it was the day of the autumn races, and the white people were at the race course which lay on the edge of the city. There was a delay of two hours, and Carie lay dying. When the doctor came he set swiftly to work upon her, directing Andrew and Wang Amah to follow his example for the sick child.

Carie was unconscious by this time, but again her good body responded, and she was able to come to herself. By ten o'clock that night she was strong enough to whisper, "Edith—Edith?"

Andrew, who could never conceal anything from her, stammered forth, "Try to believe—"

"Not dead?" gasped the poor mother.

"Yes," said Andrew helplessly.

Next day the second little coffin was bought, and Andrew alone followed it to the cemetery, and the new-made grave, the grave where Maude lay also, was opened and the third child buried there. Carie lay upon her bed, tearless, bitter, trying to humble herself before this terrifying power which thus could rob her. "I trust—after this I will be better—I will trust—" But in her heart of hearts, in that wild heart of hers that would not be crushed down, she was weeping and crying, "Trust *what?*"

After her long, weary convalescence they took a junk back again to the interior city. The house seemed too big and lonely now, with Edwin once more the only child, a boy of nine. It was hard to keep him occupied and happy. She wanted her son manly and vigorous, and there was nothing in the confined and enervating atmosphere to help him except herself, and she was too sad for him. Now that he alone was left to her she brooded over him in a passion of fear and tenderness that she herself knew was not good for him.

Underneath all the days and nights her heart was bleeding for her dead children. Andrew could go back to his work again, must go back, and she must be alone. Wang Amah was her friend and helper always, but Carie needed more now than her simplicity.

Again she went back into her old work, healing where she was able, going again to the little chapel, but when she should have spoken of God her heart was arid and silent. What did she know of God except the empty words she had been taught? There was no message on her lips. Only her obedient hands worked on.

Even when she sang the old songs she could not go through without weeping. At last her body wore out under the strain, not only the strain of her loss, but the inner strain in the quest of her life after God. She prayed often, clinging to her hope of God, because she knew of nothing else in which to believe and faith in some tangible good was essential to her positive nature. But her prayer seemed to come back to her like an echo from a call flung out into the wilderness.

Then Wang Amah, seeing her like this, went to Andrew one day when he had come home and told him that her mistress also would die if something were not done for her and done quickly. Andrew looked then at his wife. It was true that she was sad and white and thin, and the dulled look in her dark eyes frightened him.

"Carie," he said, hesitating, "shall we—would you like to go home for a while?"

She looked at him speechless, and suddenly her dark eyes filled. Home—home—it was the only thing that could save her.

They had been ten years away and according to the custom of his mission Andrew might now have a year's leave. Within a month they were once more on their way to the coast.

But in Shanghai a strange reluctance beset Carie. She did not, suddenly, want to go home. With her heart still raw and bleeding, she felt she could not bear the sympathy of the home faces and the fresh sense of bereavement. Andrew, much bewildered by this change in her, consulted a physician, and he ordered complete change of scene—"something she had never seen before." This something was the Mediterranean and Europe.

For three months they loitered through Europe, and Carie was passive as she had never been. They landed in Italy and proceeded from there to Switzerland. There they stayed a month in exquisite Lucerne and ate the golden honey and looked over the bluest of lakes to shining white mountains. It was the right medicine. Beauty restored Carie as nothing else could, and to see the beauty of cool spaces, of quiet cleanly people, of little churches with their pointed spires and great dusky cathedrals, restored her soul. Somehow the vague knowledge that life was yet good came back to her, and if good then God must still be, and sometime in the far future she must reconcile her grief to that fact. But she was too weary now for any struggle. Once she had been angry; twice she was grieved; but when her handsome, brilliant little four-year-old Edith was taken, too, she was brokenhearted, and so at last silent. The sadness of the lives of other people, also, among whom she worked had deepened the sense of sorrow everywhere. She needed to see countries where people were quietly prosperous and where suffering was not evident.

They finally wandered northward to Holland and there she eagerly sought out Utrecht and Mynheer's old furniture factory, now more modern and still a vast house of business. It was a delight to take Edwin and show him the house and the city and watch the pride in his good stout ancestry begin to grow in him. She came out of the isolation of the last ten years of her life, and was rooted in her own folk again.

Two weeks in England in late summer filled her mind full of beauty and it seemed to her she was herself again in body and somewhat healed in mind. At least she could put behind her old grief, and if she could not face the future yet she could think with excitement and joy of her own country and of her home.

Was it possible that through all these ten years this quiet plain had lain in beauty like this? Once more she sat at the window of her girlhood's room and gazed out over the old scene. There could never be enough of this quiet sitting and looking. More than music to her was it to see the hills rising wooded out of the fertile, tranquil land, to see the village street under its wide elms and maples, to go again into the small white church where Andrew's brother still ministered, his sermons somewhat more vague, his little wife rounder, and all else the same except for ten years more of life on every well-known face.

At home there were the same ones she knew and loved; her father, his hair snow white, his temper more arbitrary than ever, still stiffish with Andrew; Cornelius, married now to a black-haired pretty woman much younger than he who ruled him absolutely. All the sisters were married now, except the oldest and the youngest; and Luther—was it possible that the wild lad had grown into this prospering, thrifty business man with a wife and two babies!

Here they all were, glad to see her, tenderly sympathetic, receiving her again into the old home—and yet how widely separated was her life forever from these! Some brooding sense of difference was constantly with her, memories of other faces, stranger lands. She talked with each one of her family; they had the gay old evenings of music; she visited her sisters' homes and shared in all the details of their life, cooking, washing, cleaning house, going on long rides into the lovely autumn country in the surrey behind the two old horses—and all the time there was a part of her not there and it came to her at last that a vast chasm of knowledge of life lay between their experience and hers. They lived here safe and sheltered in a rich and fertile and new land. She knew so well now that other country, that old, old country, crowded with too many suffering people, fetid with too abundant life—life too swiftly born, too quickly dying, dark hot life.

Gradually it came to her that rooted as she was by birth and love to this country of her own, to America, yet she was bound also to China, bound by her very knowledge of it, bound by such souls as Wang Amah, bound by the three small bodies sleeping in the ancient earth and mingling at last their pale dust with its darkness. Ah, that country was no longer alien to her now. She could bear to go back one day, because some of her own flesh and spirit lay buried there.

But of going back nothing was said for several months. The glorious autumn passed—was it ever as glorious as this? All those ten years had the maples yearly flamed like this? Winter came and Christmas and every son and daughter and the children of sons and daughters gathered under the roof of the big white house. Edwin was beside himself with joy in their midst. Too excited to talk coherently he rushed through the happy days of concentrated play and in such freedom of house and woods and meadows, of snow and skating and tobagganing, as he had never dreamed were true.

"Oh, I love America, Mother!" he cried over and over. It was this cry alone that sent a pang through Carie. If she went back would she deprive him of this fair country, his birthright? Still there was the silent and sad bond between her and that other land.—No, she would not decide now.

After Christmas they went on a visit to Andrew's home, a great rambling farmhouse on the Greenbrier River. Here were folk different from her own. They lived in a lavish way as to food, and the waste was appalling to her thrifty Dutch blood, but there was always a scarcity of cash, although on the large farm fruit and produce lay wasting. Andrew's father was a tall, gaunt, somber man, with deep religious eyes, and a temper dour and mystic. His voice came forth with the solemnity of one speaking from a tomb.

Andrew's mother, on the other hand, was a humorous and sarcastic old lady, with a bitter twist to her tongue. She had decided to retire from active life when she was sixty years old, and thereafter spent her time, able-bodied as she was, in her rocking chair or in her bed, from which two points of vantage she viewed her world. The sport of her life was the constant bickering she maintained with her husband, who did not have her gift for argument, and answered her in thunderous tones until she was silent.

Every night the old man would have a fire of logs lit in the great stone fireplace and then stretch himself on the skin rug on the hearth and stare silent and glowering into the flames. What he dreamed of no one knew, but in that day when people feared the evil magic of draughts, it was a nightly hazard to lie thus before the fire. His scoffing old wife never failed to cry at him, "You'll catch your death lying there!" Or, when that proved too mild for his rejoinder, "You just act childish lying there."

She could find no content until she had nagged him long enough to see him turn to her, his shaggy grey eyebrows drawn down, and hear him thunder at her, "Silence, woman!" After which she grew gay and spoke no more to him except to snort at intervals through the evening when her eyes rested on him.

From this marriage and out of this severe, unjoyous home had come seven sons and two daughters, all the sons except one choosing the ministry as their profession. To Carie it seemed a strange home, one having none of the small graces and courtesies of life which made her own so pleasant a place. But from her visit there, which she made as brief as she could, she understood Andrew better, his austerities, his shynesses, his fires so deep and so strangely banked, the powerful mystic motive of his life.

In the late autumn she had known that again she was to bear a child and now it seemed to her that she must stay in her own old home until this little life was begun. So she went back to her room to wait and through the beautiful American spring she lived, refusing to think of what was past or of what must come, sharing with Edwin the delight of sowing and of early fruitage, finding a dream-like pleasure in the plucking of apples from a tree in June, of eating strawberries and cherries still wet with dew, silvery and cool with the morning.

She gave herself wholly now to this simple and perfect life, content to think no more until the child was born. The very tasks of this life were joy, the washing of clothes under the trees in the back yard where the tubs were put under a great elm tree and the kettle hung upon crossed iron legs, and the water pumped deep and clear from the nearby well; the ironing of the snowy clothes in the coolness of the buttery, with the door open to the green garden and a bee buzzing about as one worked; churning and seeing the butter gather in golden grains first upon the creamy surface of the milk, and then collect themselves into the solid golden mass, molding the butter fats, fresh and salted, and stamping each with the old strawberry stamp.

Edwin was in everything, insisting on his share in every activity, but breaking away every now and again to romp barefoot with his cousins through the orchard and meadows. It did Carie more good than anything to see him lose the paleness that the Orient had set upon him and see him grow big and ruddy and clear-eyed, and more noisy and joyous than she had thought he ever could.

Best of all were the quiet Sabbath mornings and breakfast so late in the big cool dining room that even Hermanus was there. Over the very house, spotless from Saturday cleaning, hung the atmosphere of stillness and reverence. Then came the slow walk to church dressed in one's fresh best, her father's beloved white head at the front of the line of family proceeding up the shady village street; there were dignified friendly greetings from neighbors, the music of the church bell—sweetest music to Carie—and then the still beauty of holiness in the quiet church. Surely there was God, almost made visible.

In such ways of peace and beauty did Carie's country heal her. And then, with no sign, with no sudden vision, the consciousness of her old purpose came floating back into her heart. Here so much of beauty and cleanliness, of beauty and righteousness; over there the dark empty hands and broken bodies, the more pathetic irresistible call of the pitiful to her too tender heart.

With no sign then, with no sudden visions yet from God, but with only the long silent call of the unhappy and, to her, the somehow unsaved, she knew she must go back.

Her little daughter was born to her on a cloudless summer's day, and when the hour was over, she turned on her bed to look out over the plains to the hills, and from somewhere the goodness of life came flooding back into her heart. Life again—this little life lying here beside her —what name could she give the child better than this, her little Comfort? Thus she named the child.

They stayed four more months until the baby was well started on her way, and by this time she had become the center of the home. Every day the little girl cousins washed her clothes proudly and brought them upstairs freshly ironed and smelling sweet of sun and wind. They were all proud of the baby's fair prettiness in a family where eyes were commonly dark, and to the mother Comfort became hope also.

With this little Comfort, she told herself, she could even leave her land again; with this little American daughter, born in her own home, she could go back to that other land. If fear sometimes beset her, thinking how swiftly those other little lives had come and gone, still she knew she must go even for Andrew's sake, for he was chafing to be away and at work.

Yes, she must go. Had it taken the death of the other three to break her to God's will, His silent will? She was broken, then, and she would do that will. She would ask for no more signs from God. She would only trust and obey, now, and she could but obey the call, if not of God, seeing that He did not speak, at least of those in that other country, those less happy, less fortunate, the oppressed by life. Perhaps it was even so that God spoke.

But whether He spoke or not she would obey and "go into all the world."

Back again then over land and sea she went. There was fear of the sea in her heart and a rush of dreadful memory when the old seasickness robbed her of her milk for the baby so that she had to be put on artificial food. Nor would the baby consent to take the bottle, being by nature an individual small in body but mighty in will, and one of Carie's humorous memories of this journey was Andrew, holding in his big awkward hands this cheerful but determined infant, feeding her perilously from a cup with a spoon. So she was fed across the Pacific Ocean by the combined efforts of Andrew and the stewardess, fortunately a kind woman who conceived an affection for the obstinate, smiling mite.

But this baby throve in spite of all and was carried ashore in Shanghai vigorous and gay and apparently unmoved by ten thousand miles of travel before she was six months old. She was just the sort of baby Carie needed, a funny, round, humorous child, bursting with small demands and good cheer. Wang Amah had been told of the arrival and had come to the coast, and her beaming face with its hanging lower lip was the first Carie saw as she stepped on the pier. The good old brown creature rushed to Edwin and hugged him to her bosom much to his manly disgust. Then she received into her arms the little, fair, round girl, and to her it was the two dead babies back again, and she clutched the little thing, laughing and weeping. When Carie would have taken the child herself for the riksha ride to the hotel Wang Amah would not give her up. As for Comfort, she accepted this new love as her right, staring a little at Wang Amah's dark face and strange looks, but accepting her.

They stayed but a day on the coast, for it was already late autumn and the weather was cool, and Andrew was anxious to be on his country trips again. But in that day Carie found an hour to go to the little plot of ground where her three babies lay, and there she planted the root of a white rose tree that she had brought from the porch of her home. On the day of her departure she had dug it up and wrapped it well in earth and moss and sacking, and had watered it all the way across the sea.

"These little three never saw our America, their own land," she said to Edwin sorrowfully as he helped her. "They were born and died in an alien country and it will make me happier to think that there is something of America and of our own home above them for beauty and a covering."

A great palm tree grew above the grave and under its coolness the white American rose grew and throve.

Then once more they set forth, first on a steamer up the Yangtse River and then by junk up the Grand Canal to their old place of Tsingkiangpu.

There were pangs of memory in house and garden— that dreadful ditch where Arthur had been hurt—she could not bear it and must needs fill it in and cover it with a flower bed. But she would not think now of what was past. There was this small, demanding, cheerful new presence in the house; there was Edwin to be taught; there was another American family coming to live there too, and there was a boy for Edwin to play with, and she would have a sweet and gentle American woman for a friend. And above all there were those who had called her back to them by the very silence of their need, the dark crowds who lived in the land of her return. The first time she had come for God's sake. Now she came for the sake of these.

I can now begin to tell something of this story myself, having at this time properly begun my acquaintance with this American woman. My first memories of her are in the home at Tsingkiangpu. They are very slight memories, scarcely more than softly flashing pictures, whose reality I half doubt except that they are so unchangeably fixed in my mind.

I remember one early spring morning in the court, where roses bloomed everywhere, festooned against the grey brick wall, glowing along the edge of a small green. I am clinging to Edwin's hand, staggering over the old flagged pathway. Ahead of us looms the big gate, always closed against the passing world outside. The gate is raised from the ground some six inches and underneath it marches an unceasing procession of feet—bare feet, straw-sandaled feet, velvet-shod feet. These are for me the outer and unknown world. I stop, and very carefully, for I am somewhat obese, I lower myself to the ground and peer under the gate. But all my peering brings me no higher vision than flowing robes knee high or to the feet, or bare brown legs on which the muscles stand out like ropes. I can make nothing of it and rise again, dusting myself.

Just then she comes out, the person around whom our own inner world revolves. She is dressed in a ruffly white dress that sweeps the grass as she walks and she has a big, old straw hat with a red ribbon tied around it on her curly brown hair. She has a pair of garden shears and she goes snipping the roses, wet with dew as they are, until she has a great armful.

One perfect white rose, as large, it seemed to me, as a plate, she holds at arm's length, gazing at it. It is covered with shining drops of water. At last she puts it to her nostrils delicately, and seeing the look of ecstasy on her face, I clamor also for this privilege. Whereupon she extends the rose to me and recklessly I bury my face in it. It is larger and wetter even than I had thought, and I emerge from it sneezing and gasping and drenched, with all the sensations of having been suddenly submerged in a cold pool.

One whole summer it seems to me I scarcely saw her at all. She lay day and night on her bed, shrunken very small and thin, and her eyes enormous. Once in the morning and once at night Wang Amah leads me in to see her. I have always a fresh white dress put on me first, and my yellow hair is curled in a long Thames tunnel on the top of my head, this being made perfect over Wang Amah's dark forefinger, her tongue hanging out of her mouth as she works. When her tongue goes back into her mouth I know it is finished and I may move again. Indeed, during this whole summer Wang Amah looms far more important to me than any other. She bathes me, feeds me, croons the curliest of Chinese tunes to me, stocks my mind well with Chinese rhymes, scolds me to heaven for undue independence, and twice a day prepares me for the rite of going into the other one's, the white one's, room.

Long afterwards, when Carie would tell over again the story of those days, I knew that she had fallen victim again to one of the dreaded intestinal germs of dysentery, and for three long months she lay on her bed—all through the hot summer. She had, she said, to give the children to Wang Amah to care for, and though Edwin was a big boy, Comfort was only two. She feared every day for the baby, but twice a day Wang Amah brought her in, spotless and fresh and cool, her hair newly brushed and curled, and her little face happy and good-natured.

There was no doctor there in those days, but a friend of Carie's, one of the many to whom at some time she had been kind, an Englishwoman who was also a physician, heard of her plight and left her own work and station and instead of taking her vacation, came and nursed Carie and treated her throughout the summer. Otherwise Carie would surely have died, for again she was with child.

The passing of the great heat in September brought with it one cooling, windy morning a little son whom she named Clyde, a black-haired, blue-eyed, fat little boy. Carie, seeing the rounded healthy child, marvelled that her own wasted frame could have borne such a fruit of health and strength. The cool weather brought new healing to her, however, and her magnificent body rallied yet again.

These were, on the whole, happy years for her. She gradually took up again her work among the people, opened again her little clinic for mothers and babies, her classes for reading, and received again the many who came to her for help of one sort and another. But with all this she did not leave the children. The clinic was held in the gate house, and she taught and talked in a room in the house from where she could look out of the window to the children as they played in the court.

This work she did in the afternoons. In the morning she must teach Edwin, for he was a big lad now, and quick for his years, and before she knew it Comfort was clamoring to learn to read. Her three children thus grew apace, strong and well and keen of brain. They were children who delighted in music and color. She had to devise many things for them, this American mother, who had to supply in her own nature and resource the whole American environment that was their heritage. Especially did she think at this time of Edwin, growing into a tall boy, finishing always too easily for his own good his lessons and the tasks she set for him. She did not want him to have too much leisure, too much time to wander about the streets. The American family from whom she hoped much stayed but a short time, and again she was Edwin's only companion. Her constant fear was that she would not be able to keep her children to the standards of life and thought in their own country, that in spite of her the languid Oriental acceptance of things as they were would creep into her children's souls and enervate them.

The only real quarrel she ever had with Wang Amah was on this score. Carie, seeing that Edwin disliked to bestir himself physically, set him the task of carrying in the kindling wood for the stoves each day and in addition the task of keeping his own room clean and tidy. To Wang Amah this was sacrilege. The eldest son—compelled to do the work of a menial in the house—it was unthinkable! While the family was eating breakfast, she would creep into Edwin's room and swiftly set it to rights, and when young Edwin came in, there was his room, shining and spotless and his work done for him. He kept a discreet silence until one day Carie discovered Wang Amah at her guilty service of love.

Carie had a swift temper and at times a sharp tongue, and by now a very complete command of the Chinese vernacular. Moreover, where her children were concerned she would brook no interference, especially where she conceived their training and righteousness to be. She spoke her mind to Wang Amah, and the gentle old woman replied apologetically, "It is a shameful thing in our eyes to make the eldest son work. For the girls, yes, it is well, but not for the sons."

"Yes!" cried Carie indignantly, "and so your men grow idle and devilish like that one from whom I took you!"

It was complete answer, and Wang Amah crept away stricken. Later Carie, swiftly repentant as ever, tried to explain that boys must be taught to work if they are to achieve anything and that in America boys and girls are taught alike and valued alike. But this was a social order beyond Wang Amah's comprehension, although never again did she protest.

Much of the effort of Carie's life, then, at this time was put into shaping her oldest son. In a country where the whole environment tended to give him a false and exalted opinion of himself, it was hard to teach him courtesy to his mother and sister and to the Chinese women who came as visitors. Edwin was a high-tempered boy, moreover, and the servants treated him too deferentially and he heard talk of his place as the oldest son, and all this Carie found difficult to counteract. Andrew was continuously away from home, and when he came in for brief intervals of rest was too weary to take time to enter the boy's life.

I have as a souvenir of this period of her life a little newspaper which at her suggestion he compiled every week, a little sheet illustrated with a remarkably clever pen and ink sketch he made of a junk. The junk is full sail and leaping with the wind—it is, in fact, a very spirited and living drawing. This newspaper was Carie's idea, but Edwin, whose natural bent was to writing and drawing, took it up eagerly. He collected items of news from various places, sent out advertisements to widely

scattered mission stations and ports and actually found
not a few subscribers, some of whom doubtless were glad
to help the boy with a few pennies a month. He accumulated this way some pocket money which, I am afraid,
in spite of Carie's vigilance, he spent on such delicacies as
fried Chinese noodles and sesame candy sticks and little
larded cakes sold by the traveling vendors on the street.

But if Edwin was a continual problem to her he was
a joy as well. As for Carie, I have it from Edwin that
she filled an astonishing place in his life. His memory of
her is of a joyous, cheerful, interesting companion, with
unfailing ideas of something to do. At any moment those
gold-flecked eyes of hers would kindle and she would cry
out, "I tell you what let's do!"

And there was always something delightful. She taught
him to sing and to play the violin, and was a never fail-
ingly sympathetic although severe critic of his attempts
at writing a novel and an epic poem. Novels, it is true,
she did not encourage. As a matter of fact, there was
nothing she secretly enjoyed more than a good novel, for
she was human to her heart's core and the doings of
people interested her more than anything. But she had
been taught by the religion of her times that novels were
evil and must be put with dancing and card-playing, and
it was typical of the division in her nature that she could
laugh in purest pleasure over *Pickwick Papers* and then
feel a little guilty that she thought it funny. She compro-
mised somewhat by having no novels in the house except
classics, and to this at least her children owed the fact
that they early formed a taste for nothing but the best.
Edwin at seven was poring over Dickens and Thackeray
and Scott, as later the other children did also, and forever
after, having eaten strong meat, they found lesser writers
pallid and tasteless.

Seven children never taught Andrew how to hold a
baby or how to dress a child. He was born prophet and
saint, a man far from the daily life of mankind. Even in
his own home there was a quality of remoteness about
him. No child of his thought of running to him to have

a shoe tied or a button fastened. I have heard Carie laugh and say, "It was the funniest thing sometimes when I was sick and he had to help Wang Amah with the children a little. He would bring them in with their little clothes fastened back side before. They looked so strange—one didn't know whether they were coming or going!"

He was a man like Saint Paul, indeed, to whom he has been likened by many; a man by nature religious and a pioneer, in many things fearless, devoted to his duty as he conceived it, seeing nothing else. To his children he was a figure always a little dim, living outside their world. He was very strict with them when he thought of them, truly desiring their righteousness above all else, yet through some lack of understanding never able to make righteousness beautiful to them. They preferred their mother's swift impetuosities, her sudden little tempers and warm instant apologies, her great close embraces and her little jokes and merry looks to all the cool goodness of their father.

Yet in justice to Carie it must be said that she never herself doubted the importance of the primacy of Andrew's mission. However impatient she might be sometimes with the hardships it laid upon her, I think she felt secretly that there was in his mysticism something too high for her and for us to understand, and we must just follow behind. It was about this time, for instance, that I remember the shadow of what we called "Father's New Testament." Andrew had a keen and critical literary sense and he had for long been dissatisfied with the only translation which had been made of the Bible into Chinese. Gradually through the years there shaped in his mind the idea of making a translation at least of the New Testament and this directly from the Greek into Chinese. He was an excellent Greek scholar, and always in his own personal devotions read the Bible in the original Hebrew and Greek. I can remember the faded gilt edge of the small pocket edition of the Greek Testament he carried in the breast pocket of whatever suit he wore. When he died and we laid him to sleep for his eternity, we knew he could not rest unless it were with him still, and we put it there forever.

So he began to work on the translation in the evenings or during his few days of vacation in the summer, and as the years passed, the pile of manuscript, covered with the long lines of his somewhat angular Chinese writing, grew higher upon the desk in his study. One of the members of our household came to be the old, stooped Chinese scholar who came often at his request to consult with him about style and phrases.

But the day came when the work was finished and must be published, and there was no money to publish it except what we could spare from our already too meager salary. They talked it over, Carie and Andrew, she thinking of her children and he of his book. She said, "But, Andrew, the children can't have less clothing than they have now—I turn and patch and remake, and I dare not cut down on their food."

"I know," he said, despairing and longing.

Then she looked at him and saw what it meant to him, and how it was his dream, and so at last she said, "We will do it somehow. Every month take five dollars away and set it aside, and we will do on what is left. I must cut down a penny or two anywhere I can."

He was happy again, although thereafter the children came to think that Father's New Testament was a sort of well down which were lost the toys they longed for, or a new dress a little girl hoped for, or the many books for which they hungered. They learned to ask wistfully, "Mother, when Father is finished the New Testament, may we buy something we want?" They will never forget their mother's face when they asked this question. She looked angry, but not at them, and she said very firmly, "Yes! We will each one of us buy the thing we want most."

But we never did, for she died before Andrew ever finished. He printed edition after edition, revising each to make it more perfect, and all her life she went poorer because of the New Testament. It robbed her of the tiny margin between bitter poverty and small comfort. Still she never let the children's wistfulness deepen into complaint. She had made a decision and shaped her life to it, and she compelled respect for Andrew's dream, even when she rebelled, sometimes not too secretly, against it.

Yet it was impossible for the children not to realize a great difference in their parents. One of the questions which long continued in Comfort's mind as a small girl was this: her father came to breakfast every morning with three red marks graven upon his high white forehead. The marks faded gradually during the morning, but when he first came in to the meal as he bent his head to ask grace they were very red and severe. One day she took courage to ask Carie, "What makes the red marks on Father's forehead?"

"They are the marks of his fingers where he leans his head on his hand to pray," Carie answered soberly. "Your father prays for a whole hour every morning when he gets up."

Such holiness was awe-inspiring. The children looked for like marks of it on their mother's forehead, and one asked, "Why don't you pray, too, Mother?"

Carie answered—was it with a trifle of sharpness?— "If I did, who would dress you all and get breakfast and clean house and teach you your lessons? Some have to work, I suppose, while some pray."

Andrew came out of his habitual abstraction long enough to overhear this, and to remark gently, "If you took a little more time for prayer, Carie, perhaps the work would go better."

To which Carie replied with considerable obstinacy, "There isn't but so much time and the Lord will just have to understand that a mother with little children has to condense her prayers."

The truth of it was that Carie was not very good at long prayers. She prayed hard and swiftly at times, but she prayed as she worked, and she was always perhaps a little conscious against her will that her voice seemed to go up and come back to her without surety of reply. But during this middle period of her life she purposely pushed into the background of her busy life the old striving after a realization of God. Passive she was not and never could be, but she was sure of only one thing and it was that she must do what she could to help anyone who came near her and who needed help—her children, her neighbors, her servants, the passersby. Her religion she finally wrapped into three words, "Trust and obey." She simply had to take God on trust if He were there at all, and she would act as though He were there and would do the practical things that make any religion of social worth. I think in no part of her life was she more typically American than in the mental doubt and secret unsurety of her theoretical beliefs and in the swift and responsive generosities of her nature.

The only times Edwin drew near to his father at all were when he had been exceptionally restless at home and in despair Carie urged Andrew to take the boy with him on his country trips occasionally. The two went together by junk and on mule-back across miles of country, and in the enforced comradeship of shared meals and in the seclusion at evening of being the only two of their kind, Edwin understood for the first time what his father was really about, and for the first time this passion for the welfare of people's souls was dimly beautiful to him.

The influence of these two, then, his father with his love for the souls of men and his mother with her passionate warm interest in the human welfare of men and women, was to make him forever dissatisfied with any work that had as its sole end the making of money. His mother's natural skepticism, which she subdued in herself all her life by the most strenuous effort of will, flowered in him and in his times, so that he could never return to a religious mission, but there was the subtler influence that shaped him irrevocably so that he saw humanity first above all else and was instant to respond to their needs.

Meanwhile Andrew had come to one of his periodic conclusions that he must penetrate yet farther into the interior where none had yet gone to preach the gospel, and he told Carie that again he "felt the call."

Carie heard this with the utmost dismay. This house and court had become home to her. Here were her flowers, here space for her children to live and grow. The dark city was all about her, but she had learned to accept it and she had made in the midst of it this oasis of an American home. She was one who somehow could invest her very belongings with a sense of her personality. Her garden, her rooms, her workbox, her chair—all somehow looked her own and part of herself.

Before these roots she had begun to put down deep, were others as deep. She had her friends, Chinese women who were drawn to her by their need and her response, or were drawn by the friendliness which allowed them to wander at will through her home and look at the magic of stoves and sewing machine and organ and all the wonders of a foreign land. These women Carie had learned to love, forgetting as she did so easily their differences in race and background. Moreover, two more white families were to come and she looked forward to two more friends of her own kind. But these rootings in a place and in a group which she loved made Andrew restless. He felt too many workers were gathering in one place—he must push off into new fields.

Carie expostulated, begged, was very angry, even wept a little, and then suddenly capitulated. Well she knew by now that there is nothing so adamant as a man of God when he thinks he hears his God speak. In stony silence she packed her possessions and dug up the roots of her roses, and Wang Amah put her own things into a bedding roll and a large blue kerchief, and they were ready.

IV

ANDREW had chosen a small city well to the north of them as his new base. But the people there were hostile to foreigners and would offer no house for rent and so at last Andrew took his family into an inn and there they lived in three wretched rooms, earth-walled, and with thatch for a roof and beaten earth for floor. All about them, separated only by a low earthen wall, lived the crowds of common people, packed in sordid filth.

Carie planted her roses in pots and set herself bravely to make yet again an American home. But some virtue had gone out of her. The strangeness was breath of life to Andrew and a challenge to his soul, but to her the new beginning in such surroundings, the crowded rooms and no garden space, the immanence of disease and filth, above all the dark hostility of the people, were dreadful. The memory of her three dead children came strong upon her again. Their lives so swiftly over had come to mean for her sacrifices to Andrew and to Andrew's God. She watched jealously these three yet left to her—no more sacrifices!

But to Andrew it was a year of exhilarating opportunity, although it was a year also of great hardship for him. It was a time of war with Japan, and in these remote districts every foreign face was held to be Japanese. One morning as Carie and the children sat at breakfast, not having seen Andrew for many weeks, he walked in unexpectedly. He had only his undergarments on, and he was barefoot and bleeding from wounds on his shoulders and back. He had been robbed of all he had, his mule and his traveling gear and supplies, and had been hacked by a band of wandering soldiery who insisted in spite of his protests that he was Japanese—this, although Andrew was six feet tall, blue-eyed, and in those days wore a reddish beard!

During the winter the thatched earthen house proved to be dangerously damp and the baby Clyde developed a cold which ended in pneumonia. Andrew was, as usual, away, and there was no doctor within many hundreds of miles, and Carie went through the old sickening terror of death. She hung blankets about one corner of the room and made a little spot where draughts could not reach, and behind this shelter she and Wang Amah never ceased their vigil for ten long days, and at last, as though himself unwilling, the little languid boy began the long pull back to life again.

Holding him to her, Carie cried fiercely to her heart that it was enough—it was enough! In all that city there was not one who cared whether this little son of hers lived or died in the cause of Andrew's God. Did God Himself care? . . . She would have no more sacrifices of her children.

Grimly she began to pack her goods and to prepare to leave the hovel. It had been raining for days and water had welled up on the earthen floor so that they had had to put boards on bricks to walk on. Tables and chairs stood inches in water, but the beloved organ had been hoisted onto a board platform. Now she packed everything and waited for Andrew's return. When he came in one early spring morning, she saw him coming and hurried to put on her hat and coat and met him thus to his complete astonishment, the furniture tied in mats and the roses once more dug up. She would not brook one word from him. For once she silenced him, her eyes golden and terrible in her wrath.

"You can preach from Peking to Canton," she said in a dreadful still voice, "you can go from the North Pole to the South, but I and these little children will never go with you again. I shall take them to Chinkiang to that bungalow on the hill, and if it is empty we will stay there where there is peace and where there are hills and fresh air. Otherwise I go back to our own country. I have offered up three children. I have no more children to give away to God now."

Andrew was thoroughly shocked but he could do nothing with her, for she was marching out of the gate, Edwin's hand in hers, and Wang Amah carrying Clyde and holding Comfort's hand. For once Andrew could only follow her, and they went to the canal's edge and engaged a junk and started south. She maintained her white-lipped determination until they reached Chinkiang after a journey of nearly three weeks. By great good fortune the bungalow was empty and without a word she settled into it.

In this city she made her home for twenty-seven years, and no one could move her away from it again.

The change to the hills did not, however, rid Carie of the chief problem of that time of her life, and this was again Edwin. Once more when they were settled and at peace the boy grew restless and lonely, without companions of his own age and race. He was ready for college and mature for his fifteen years, and it soon appeared to Carie that she must send him back to America alone. This decision was reached the more readily because she was anxious to have the impress of real America upon him before he grew completely to manhood. Death it was again to her heart, a new sacrifice for a cause never too clearly seen, but she had learned now to hold to the purpose of her life and see it whole, and in the coming summer Edwin was sent with friends to America.

Carie wrote long, pleading letters to her brother Cornelius, commending her boy to his care, so that every holiday she could think of him there in the big house, in that quiet and good atmosphere. It was a comfort to her after he was gone, but in spite of it there were many long nights when she lay awake in agony, reproaching herself that she had sent him away so young. He who had seemed like a young man when he stood beside her, when he was away was a child again. She wrote him long letters full of love and eagerness, trying to feel from him all that he was thinking and doing. When she heard he had learned to smoke she went wretched for days, fearing he had learned other things too. But Cornelius sent favorable reports of the tall lad, and these she read with pride. At the end of the letter he remarked guardedly, "Edwin we find is a little lazy." Then Carie was glad her son was out of the idle, dreamy atmosphere of the East and into the keen sharp life of his own country. It was well for him—it was well for him—but her home seemed half empty!

The bungalow on the hills was not to be hers for long. The family to whom it belonged came back from a furlough, and again they had to move. This time Andrew found a small house in the Chinese city, but fortunately on the edge of it so that with little difficulty Carie could take the two children to the hills every day for fresh air.

But the house stood near the Bund, on the land the Chinese were forced to give by treaty to the British after the Opium wars, and the district was filled with the resorts of disreputable persons. Hurrying her children past the open doors in which sat lounging half-dressed women of every breed, Carie was grateful beyond words that

Edwin was not there, Edwin with his sharp, adolescent eyes. White men from the ships were hanging about these brothels, and to Carie this was infinitely dreadful, so much more dreadful than if there had been only Chinese. It gave her a sense of shame and hopelessness that out of her fair country, of which she was so proud, should come these two together, Andrew with his clear flame of righteousness, and these tipsy, cursing, lecherous men. Yet her heart rushed out to them too, for often they were young, sometimes almost as young as her own son, and they were all far from home; and if they were old, then they had been exiled so long that they were homeless now on the earth, and that was yet more sad.

Once again she took up her old service and watched for the ships coming in from other lands and she cooked and baked and filled her little house with sailors and marines and listened to their hungry confidences and supplied the need to many for mother and sister and friend.

Carie in these days had particular delight in Clyde, for of all her children he was the one most like her and most closely knit to her spirit. He grew into a most exceptionally brave and handsome child, his temper at once grave and gay, and like her he had a heart too warm for its own good. To his mother he turned instinctively like a flower to the sun, and they seemed saturated with happiness when they were together.

Her courageous heart she had given to him, and I never saw her more moved than on one day when he was nearly five years old and Andrew whipped him sorely for some chidish mistake—a hard, spare hand Andrew had—and Clyde after his brief fit of crying began to sing stoutly, "Onward, Christian Soldiers," his eyes still wet with tears and his little thighs marked and sore. For years after when he was only a memory, she thought of his little wet face, blue eyes big and brave, and his little quivering voice, and the tears would rush to her own eyes. He had her love of beauty and I remember how with a great shout he ran to greet the first dandelions of spring, and how every spring after he died she gathered handfuls of dandelions and made his grave gay with them because he loved them so well.

For this beloved child, when he was little more than five years old, was taken one day with a high fever, and soon was desperately ill. There was no doctor in the city except an Indian half-breed, a gentle, kindly man with no great medical skill, and the British customs doctor, a man so continually drunk that no one knew what his ability was. The Indian pronounced the disease bronchitis, but from the first Carie feared diphtheria, for by now she had considerable practical knowledge of medicine from her own study and experience with the Chinese who came to her for help.

She watched unceasingly but Clyde grew rapidly worse and she sent a runner for Andrew, three days away in the country. At last the little fellow's throat choked completely and it was evident that nothing could save him. Before Andrew could reach home the child died, and once more Carie held a son dead in her arms.

Andrew reached home in time to see his fair little son in his coffin. On the next day, the day of the funeral, the wind blew a great gale and the rain fell unceasingly and Carie, worn and ill herself, and bearing within her again another life, was not able to follow the little cortege to the small plot where white people lay dead.

Ah, the infinite pathos of those little squares of land that lie scattered through such Chinese cities here and there, the little squares of land where white and alien people have prepared for themselves a small space where they may lie dead! They are always enclosed in high walls, these spaces, and the gates are tall and spiked with iron and locked with great iron bars. Within the strange quiet there are a few trees and sanded paths arranged in orderly fashion, and the graves lie close, most of them graves of women and little children—many, many little children; seamen's graves, too, and always the graves of those who, the epitaphs say, were murdered at the hands of angry mobs. But if all these were alien on this

Chinese soil when they were alive, they are no less alien dead; no, more when dead. It is as though they protected themselves thus lest even dead they might be swallowed up by the encroaching, careless, teeming multitudes about them.

I remember on the day they buried Clyde that Carie stood at the window weeping and watching the short procession file along the walk of the court and her tears fell upon my bare heart and only half-understanding I crept to her side and gazed out. The rain fell in long lines and spattered upon the small coffin they were carrying out of the gate. When we could not see it any more she still wept on, not angrily now, not passionately, but as one weeps out of a heart grown hopeless.

Some virtue went out of Carie on that day, never to return; something of her life ceased to exist. She had wanted the others buried in the international land in Shanghai, but this little one, though dead, she could not bear to have separated from her. Since his mother's life must be lived in this far country, her little son must bear her company still.

The day after Clyde was buried, Comfort fell very ill and Carie in fresh terror saw signs of the same disease developing. Was she to have every child taken from her, then? She could not bear the sight of the Indian doctor any more with his dark, listless gaze and his languid movements. Into the rain and wind she went out, calling a sedan chair to carry her the more swiftly, to seek the tipsy port doctor. She found him in a brothel with a giggling Chinese girl upon his knee and she went swiftly to him and shook him by the shoulders to rouse him.

"My child is dying," she said simply. "It is diphtheria. Will you come?"

Some long-forgotten response to duty woke struggling through the white man's bloodshot eyes, and he staggered up, letting the girl slide to her feet, and without a word he followed Carie, muttering as he went, "I have some new stuff—lots of diphtheria—I got at Shanghai—I might try that new stuff—"

Afterwards she found that in his lucid moments he was a physician of no mean order and he had happened to get from Shanghai only the day before some of the new antitoxin. Carie dared not leave him an instant lest he lapse into insensibility, and she directed the chair-bearers to follow him to the place where he lived. There she followed him into the house, roused him when he sat down and began to nod, searched his laboratory for the small bottle he was too fumbling to find, hunted his hypodermic needle and then urged him on until she had him at last in her house and beside the sick child's bed.

There suddenly he came to himself, was unexpectedly rational and steady of hand. He administered the drug. Within a day the child was better. Two more doses and she was out of danger. Then Carie, the crisis over, came suddenly to the end of her strength, and there was no one to nurse the child back to health. Andrew, who had stayed at home until danger was over, felt now he must be on his way again to his work, and moreover had he stayed he would not have been of use, for Comfort would have none of him.

There came forward at this point one of those friends from somewhere whom Carie always seemed to have, some person to whom she had once been kind. This time it was a young English girl, ignorant and untutored, who had come as nursery governess to the family of a customs official and had become entangled in one of the sordid love affairs of port life. She had fled to Carie when at last she had to leave the house of her employer and Carie had sheltered her and helped her through until she saw her own folly and despised the man who had shamed her and was to take passage for home again. Now she postponed her going and stayed to nurse Comfort, no small task, for the child in her convalescence cried for her mother and exhibited to the full her store of determination and wilfulness. For this help Carie was most tenderly grateful, and the friendship between the two women was deepened into one of years, and continued long after Comfort was well and grown into a woman.

It seemed to Carie as though she would never feel strong and never blithe again. She stayed listless through the early winter and shuddered in the damp river chill of early spring. The house was dismal and lonely again with only one child in it, and Edwin was very far away now and absorbed in his new life. The thought of the little one to come brought no cheer, for it seemed futile to go on bearing and losing—a dreadful, heart-breaking loss and waste of life.

She went back to her old morbid fear lest it was through some sinfulness of her own that she had lost her children, some sinfulness and inner rebellion. Had she not in reality given up the old hungry quest after God and been satisfied with mere service to people? She had never tried hard enough to find God. Now it seemed to her that God might break her again and again until she was submitted to Him and she began to struggle to submit herself lest again she be broken—as long as she had one child left God might break her once more.

She began to spend more time trying to pray, and tried to still the old longing that God would give a sign that He heard. She read books of religious practice and tried to follow certain rules of praying and reading the Bible. But that impatient, practical mind of hers would outrun the words and even as she read she brooded of other things.

Beauty alone, she thought at last in a sort of despair, beauty alone might heal her; the still, remembered beauty of mists over the valleys, mountain tops, the little rows of flowers she had had in all the homes she had made; beauty of music and poetry brought a sort of peace also, and yet she feared this peace, for she was not sure it was of God, not sure that after all it might not be merely the assuaging of that pleasure-loving part of her she had always to subdue. The God of whom she had been taught all her days was austere and there was no austerity in her and she could not be healed by it.

146

When in May a little daughter came to her, a little blue-eyed, dark-haired girl, Carie could scarcely smile. Day after day passed and she seemed unable to rally from the birth. At last a fever set in and it was evident that there was a poisoning of her blood. Her milk dried and in the silent house there was the crying of the hungry newborn child. Andrew and Wang Amah between them tried to feed the little thing a milk mixture which she complained of bitterly, in spite of her hunger. But by this time the mother was past knowing what happened to the child.

Then Wang Amah saw with agony this final catastrophe. She viewed with the utmost disfavor the weak broths and watered milk dishes that the doctor prescribed for her mistress. One night, Carie told me afterwards, the broth she was fed in the night tasted strongly of fish. It was nauseous; but she supposed dimly it must have been placed next to some fish and could not actually hurt her and she needed the nourishment and so she swallowed it. But after she had eaten she felt a strange stimulation. She slept at once and more restfully than she had for many days, and awoke in the morning better, and from then on she began to recover.

Weeks after when Carie was up and well again Wang Amah told her she had not been able to bear to see her die and die she would if the white doctor was allowed to go on as he was. She brewed secretly therefore a dish of special broth made from a particular fish and herbs the Chinese use for puerperal fever, and this she substituted for the usual bowl of broth, and this Carie had drunk.

"I don't know whether that saved me or not," she used to say, "or whether the fever was ready to turn anyway. But Wang Amah's broth did not hurt me and she had a lot of wisdom of her own sort that life had taught her."

At any rate, Carie was well again, and for us all it was enough.

The following summer the bungalow on the hill was once more empty, for the family who had lived in it returned to America to stay, and now it was assigned to

Andrew and Carie for a home. To another it might have seemed a poor joy, a small, decrepit brick cottage, whose sagging floors were full of centipedes and scorpions. I remember as a regular rite every midnight during the warm weather Andrew holding the light high, and Carie, with her swift arm slapping the venomous insects dead with an old leather slipper. Centipedes lurked in the most intimate places; once Carie found a nest of them under her pillow, once Andrew squeezed a big one out of his sponge in his morning bath. But the cottage was bliss and enough for Carie. There was an old garden and old trees and a white rose bush hung over the veranda. When they moved into the house in May the rose bush was in bloom with clusters of tiny, button-like white roses, heavy and sweet with a musky fragrance. And the turtle dove had her nest there.

Here Carie set herself steadily to life again. Comfort was growing into a great girl now and must be taught in all the ways of American womanhood, and here was baby Faith. Carie could live with a full heart, moreover, for beauty was spread around her in the hills and in the little, garden-like valleys between, where small brown men and women worked at their fields; and to Carie beauty was a sort of oxygen which gave her life and energy. Here the mists rose up at dawn from the river and covered the frothing bamboos, and tall grasses grew silvery on the graves on the hills. In the valleys were round pools of water among the fields, fringed with willow trees and peach trees and in spring the beauty was as great as any she had ever seen.

Edwin's letters, too, added to her content, for he was far happier than he had been. At first he had been desperately lonely and the country she had taught him to call home seemed in spite of all alien to him. She had been filled with dismay at this, so that she thought, "It is well I sent him back when I did or he would never have grown into his own land."

And so the consciousness that she had done well by her son gave her comfort, and it was like renewing her own love of country when he began to fit into his place and to discover America for himself.

As for the four who were dead, they were never far from her. The three in Shanghai she visited when she could, and the little enclosed plot where Clyde lay was within easy walking distance and she could steal away there and sit for a little while by that small quiet grave.

Thus she set herself resolutely to this middle portion of her life, a manifold life now as it had ever been. She made again, and this time with her first sense of permanence, her home. The six rooms were large and had wide casement windows flung open to garden and valley and hill, and it was sweet to her to make a home there.

I remember that home as a place of delight to us all for its simple order and cleanliness and its grace of flowers, and the sweet smell of the grass mats on the floors is in my nostrils yet. There Comfort began to grow into womanhood and there Faith began to talk and walk and grow into girlhood. From this house Andrew went forth refreshed and encouraged for his long tours of preaching and teaching. From it, too, went out the refulgent outpouring of Carie's abundant hospitality; young American couples, bewildered with their first days in the Orient, started their life in her guest room; weary missionaries rested there; stray tramps slept there, those strange bits of wastage of the white race who are washed up casually from the great Oriental sea, who seem scarcely to know themselves how they are come, and certainly never where they are going—all those who were homeless and sad came by some unknown path to her door, and she received them and saw them started again, clean and fed and heartened.

What she said to these was not a great deal beyond the practical, merry talk she made of this and that in common affairs, for she was never any good at preaching. If there was some speech of the spirit she wished to have with someone, most often she had it through her singing —music from a favorite hymn or oratorio. She would pour it out richly, tenderly, at an hour of evening when the house was quiet and full of thought and dreaming, and without further effort would leave it to do its own work.

Once a strange tramp came to us and stayed a week. What he was no one knew, an American he said, and indeed his enunciation was that of a Yankee tradesman. But the world had dealt with him until he was scarcely to be recognized as human. He stayed and ate voraciously, listened for the most part in silence, for he could scarcely speak without oaths and he perceived in some dim fashion that such speech was not appropriate here. When he left us, rested, clean, wearing a suit of Andrew's clothes and Andrew's shoes on his feet, he hesitated at the door and at last he muttered, "Never reckoned I'd see America again—have, though, and right here, ma'am!"

At about this time in Carie's life she had left to her one whom she called her Chinese daughter. A Chinese woman whom she had succored in some time of dire need, a widow, died, leaving a little girl of ten years, named Precious Cloud. When the woman died Carie was there beside her and the mother said at the end, "There has never been one who cared for me as you have. My father did not love me who was but a girl in a house already too full. My husband never loved me who came to his house only as a second wife whom he took to mend his house when the first one died; my son does not love me. Why have you loved me, who am not of your blood and bone?"

Carie, smiling over her sad heart, replied gently, "I do not know except that the need of your heart has pulled my heart and we are the children of one Father, after all."

The woman said, "There is only one possession I can leave you, for I care for only one thing. Take my little daughter for yours and make of her a woman like yourself."

This child Carie took when the mother was dead and

for years Precious Cloud was part of the house and home. During the year she was sent to a Chinese boarding school where she was given an education in her own language, for Carie would not separate the child from her own people, since she could conceive of no greater loneliness than that. She kept Precious Cloud dressed in Chinese clothes, only she did not bind her feet. Precious Cloud was at first somewhat ashamed of those big feet of hers when at that time all girls had bound feet, but Carie took the greatest pains to make her pretty shoes and have them beautifully embroidered, much more nicely than usual, so as to show Precious Cloud that natural feet could be pretty.

When Precious Cloud was seventeen and had finished school, Carie, still following the ways of the girl's own people, betrothed her to an educated young Chinese man of whose character she was assured. She made the concession of finding out first if Precious Cloud were willing, arranging for the two young people to meet in her living room—an unheard-of thing in those days. Precious Cloud was a very pretty and gentle young woman and the young man dignified and personable, and they liked each other from the first. Carie studied their temperaments carefully, amused at this new rôle, too, of matrimonial agent, and she felt they would be happy, and so they were, after the wedding which Carie tried to make Chinese in every detail she could. Precious Cloud called Carie Mother and later her little children called her Grandmother, and so Carie took to her wide deep heart these also for her children.

She could have had many children given to her had she been able to take them. Sometimes these were tragic opportunities, indeed. Once a man stalked into the chapel where Carie was talking with some women, bearing in his arms a tall, dangling figure which he laid down on the brick floor at her feet.

"Here is our son," he said harshly. "He is as you see him and he is fit only for death. Nevertheless, if you will take him, it will save us the deed. After all, he is a son."

Carie looked at the poor creature. It was an idiot boy, helpless in every way. Much as her heart was moved she could not take the child, and so she shook her head sorrowfully and tried to tell the man of his responsibility even to such a child. But the man answered nothing, only picked up the long, pale, useless body again and strode out. To the end of her days Carie, pondering, used to say, troubled, "I wonder if after all I ought not to have taken that poor thing? Somehow, I would have managed perhaps!"

This middle portion of Carie's life went by busily and therefore happily for her, although the old youthful buoyancy in her looks and ways had settled to a quiet and peaceful repose. She had seen too much of life, too much she could not understand, yet to which she had had to resign herself and so give up her old imperious questioning of God. Merriment only came to her occasionally now, although it still came and her two little girls watched for it eagerly, and the moments when their mother was gay were for them the highlights of their life. Her humor came like a gay wind, beginning with a secret and keen sparkle of her golden brown eyes. A light seemed to radiate from her and then the children hung breathless on her words, for "something funny" always followed that laughing light, some absurd rhyme or quick twist of wit. She had a faculty for easy rhyming, and sometimes for sheer mischief would spin out one ridiculous verse after another from her head.

This made the children shout with laughter, but such complete nonsense was always painful to Andrew. He would hold up his hand in protest, at first gentle, but finally fretful. "Carie—Carie—please!" he would beseech her.

But some imp of perverse enjoyment would seize her at his protest and she would rhyme more brilliantly than ever, her face alight, ending only, when she saw it really troubled him, with a fine flourish. Or perhaps she would come home from hearing some well-meaning but stupid person speak, and she would imitate the pompous intonations, much to Andrew's horror and the children's pleasure, for the children had her flashing humor and love of a joke. She was a born mimic and when she imitated someone, became in very truth that person even almost in expression.

But such merriment she never left unchecked. Too often when the children were clapping their hands and shrieking with joy, she stopped herself, vaguely troubled, saying with sudden soberness, "It is very wrong of me to make fun of a good man like Brother Jones—such a good man. Children, you must not be like your naughty mother."

It was the old struggle between her wholesome, robust nature and the imprint upon her tender conscience of the puritan religion of her youth. She was forever struggling with herself to be what she called "good," to achieve that cool—was it also selfish?—absorption in a mystic relation to God which Andrew had.

But this American woman was never to know peace for long in her life. There came in 1900 that upheaval in China which has been called the Boxer Rebellion, when in a last desperate effort to maintain the old nation the Empress tried to rid the country of foreigners by the simple method of killing off all who were there and letting no more come in.

The royal edict went forth secretly to every province and in the summer of that year astounding reports began to come of groups of white people here and there being murdered. Carie's heart rose in defense of these two children she had left to her. She waited in utmost anxiety to see what the viceroy of their province would do.

The viceroy of Kiangsu was a man of intelligence who did not fail to see the folly of the royal edict. The Empress was a woman, ignorant, narrow and provincial. True to their hopes, the viceroy was not willing to carry out the edict and kill the white people in his demesne. Instead he made a pact with the foreign consuls that if they would send no warships into his waters he would protect the white people.

Here was partial comfort but only partial, for one could not be sure how long he would hold to his promise or whether it were indeed a trap, and seeing the white people defenseless, he might plan to kill them the more easily. Andrew and Carie held long consultations with their Chinese friends. Andrew was for putting their faith wholly in God and staying on. Carie had the memory of four times when faith had not saved her babies. But they decided to stay on from day to day.

Andrew hired an old Christian man who had a junk on the river and bade him remain at a certain place near the end of a street dipped into the river. To this spot Carie planned a direct and secret route so that at any moment they could run with the children and Wang Amah down through the bamboos at the back of the house, through the reeds of the ponds and valleys to the city.

Night and day through that hot summer they were ready for the possible moment, a small basket of food for the baby, extra shoes for each person and a change of underwear rolled together. Carie packed also in a small box some possessions she valued, a little silver that had belonged to her grandfather, a cluster of amethysts set in silver by her father, some books of her mother's, and these she buried in the earth in the cellar, with the help of the manservant.

Meanwhile Carie was determined that the children should catch no shadow of the fear that was everywhere. She would not have them marred and their youthful spirits darkened by the shadows of this land in which they must live. She had always tried to make as bright and as normal a childhood for them as they could have had in their own land. So they played happily through the summer days of this year, their mornings filled with the things she devised for them to do while she did her work about the house. She played with them, too, and they remember that companionship to this day. She had more time than she had ever had, for there were not many callers. People were fearful of what the times might bring, and if the Empress were against the foreigners then one could not be seen associating with the Americans.

But a few faithful ones still came and these Carie valued, for well she loved anything that was brave and courageous. It stirred some inherited nobility in her to tell them simply that they must stand fast in their faith, as they all must, if the hour of persecution came to them, for so others had done before them. So she herself could do, and the strength of pioneer blood in her veins made her quiet and strong and fearless. She was always like this when hardship came and there was something to be borne.

At last the American consul who lived in the Bund had reason to fear treachery and he sent them word that they were to watch for the consulate flag, which they could see from their veranda. If danger became imminent he would fire a cannon and the flag would dip three times, the American flag above the consulate. This was the sign. They were to leave the house without an instant's delay and go at once to the river's edge and go aboard a steamer that would be waiting there for them. All other white people were already gone.

Carie now had to face the pulling of her heart in two. Here were her own children and the impulse of her heart was to flee with them to safety. But the little circle of Chinese friends and Christians was in a panic of fear. They had been separated from their people spiritually to some extent and now knew not what was to become of them. It was the old call to Carie, the irresistible call to her sympathy.

So it was agreed that when the sign came Carie should take the children and Wang Amah and go, while Andrew would stay behind to reinforce the people. Carie agreed to this, feeling, I think a little wistfully, that after all Andrew was "better" than she was, who was too often impatient and impetuous even when she would be kind. These weeks spent in the possible presence of death had a very sobering effect on her. She realized anew that her old nature was still strong within her even after all her sorrow, and that the early quest of her life after God was yet unfinished. This made her very humble and silent, for when the end came, if come it must, how could she point people to God, the God whom she had not found fully for herself?

Humbly, therefore, when the sign came on a humid Saturday afternoon in August, she took the two little girls and Wang Amah and with Andrew they walked through back streets as quickly as they could to the steamer. She went aboard and turned to see Andrew standing on the shore. She had more reverence for him at that moment than she had ever had, perhaps, a lonely foreign figure in his white clothes and pith helmet, tall and white among the crowd of small dark figures about him on the wharf. Whether she was ever to see him again or not she did not know.

Eight months passed, Andrew at his post and she with the two children in a small room in a Shanghai boarding house. She taught them regularly every day, and for recreation they all went to a little park that bordered a narrow space on the Whangpoo River. There the children played in the best air the close city afforded, and the joys of the day were the ships and the junks and the sampans plying in the waters. Sometimes a great ocean liner would steam majestically past the dock and that was a rich moment for all of them. Carie would draw the children to her and point it out—a ship straight from America— from home! Wang Amah stared, and the two children gazed with dreaming eyes. Neither of them knew yet what America was except for dreams that stood in their eyes of endless beauty—pink apple blossoms spreading under a blue sky, cool autumn grapes to be plucked and eaten "just so," without washing, apples on the ground you could have for the picking up, horses to ride, meadows to race in, maple sugar from the great trees that turned gold in the autumn—all this and how much more was America, their own! On such days when these ships passed, they put aside their play and asked of Carie a thousand questions about their land, and when they went back to the narrow room in the boarding house, they enlarged it with their talk and their dreams of a wide, wide country that belonged to them.

Ten months passed and the expedition sent by the western nations against the Chinese made safe the return to the bungalow on the hill, and that was a happy day when they could be together again. The house and the garden were untouched, although the little box of valuables Carie had buried was rifled, she always supposed by the manservant who helped her dig the hole. She had her moment of good indignation, but as usual such moments were followed by compunction, and she said, "Well, poor thing, I suppose he thought someone would get it, and if someone, why not he?"

This attitude of hers toward a fault she abhorred was characteristic. She hated the fault none the less as time went on, rather more even, but some largeness in her made her understand it even while she hated, and while she grew exceedingly sharp at discovering when she was being cheated. I remember as an example of this a Chinese assistant of Andrew's who that winter after her return came one day for his salary. Andrew was not at home and in his absence Carie said she would give him his money. She went upstairs to her little private safe and brought down the silver in dollars and gave it to the man. Then one of the children called and she left him for a moment. When she returned he said, "Madam, one of the dollars you gave me was bad. Will you change it, please?"

He held out in his hand a dollar obviously leaden. Quicker than a thought Carie took it and felt of it. I was warm. The dollars she had brought down were icy cold from a cold room. This dollar was warm through with the heat of the man's body.

"You are mistaken," she said quietly. "This is a dollar you have had on your person."

She looked at him steadfastly, and her eyes filled with pity.

"My friend," she said sadly, "Even for a dollar will you thus rob yourself of your honesty?"

The man's eyes fell and he was silent and went away. But she was grieved because she had thought him true.

But I have gone too quickly into the winter, for that autumn before had brought a trial of its own. Every year after the summer a plague of cholera swept the land and every year Carie lived in terror until it was past, watching with the utmost care the cooking of food and the boiling of water. Cholera in those days before its treatment was fully understood was a disease so swift and so deadly that once it was caught death followed too fast, oftentimes, for any aid to be given. In the autumn of this year Wang Amah came down with it suddenly one night and lay without calling her mistress, being reluctant to wake her from sleep.

But the sound of Wang Amah's retching and groaning wakened Carie, who was always a light sleeper, and had learned in this land of surprises to sleep, as she said, "half awake." She rose instantly and padded barefoot, in the way she had at night, being always too impetuous to stop for slippers, although this was dangerous haste in a place where centipedes abounded, to Wang Amah's room. A great terror seized her at the sight there. Wang Amah was fast sinking into unconsciousness. Then her valiant anger came to her aid as it always did. She simply would not have Wang Amah die! She sped to the kitchen stove and swiftly built a roaring fire and heated an immense tub of water. Then she poured hot water and whiskey down Wang Amah's throat, and chafed her hands and fed and administered what drugs she had. The moment the bath was hot she lifted Wang Amah into it and immersed her except her face, and then she poured milk and water into Wang Amah's mouth, manipulating her throat to make her swallow. With this stern treatment by dawn Wang Amah had come to, very feeble, indeed, but alive.

Carie called Andrew then, for she had not stopped in her haste to call anyone, and bade him stand at a distance for fear of infection, and then she gave him directions about the children and begged him now to exercise every practical power he had.

"Don't take time for your praying this morning, Andrew," she pleaded. "The children will get into all sorts of trouble before breakfast." Andrew looked at her reproachfully but in silence and it is to his honor that for a whole week he tried faithfully to follow her insturctions, shouted to him from the end of the garden where she removed Wang Amah to a little room kept usually for garden tools.

After the week Wang Amah could be disinfected and brought back to her own room and Carie could come back to the children again. Thereafter the bond between these two women was closer than ever. Wang Amah could never forget that Carie had left the children to care for her and had risked her own life in the contagion. She asked Carie, wondering, "What woman are you and what a heart is this that for a common brown creature like me whom none other has ever cared to see twice, you would give your life?"

Carie was always abashed by worship and now in her humility she confessed to Andrew that she was afraid that if she had thought about it she would never have done it, but it made her suddenly angry to see a filthy disease like cholera take Wang Amah, and she did not stop to think. Her anger was a battle call to her.

"I am afraid I did not do it for the Lord's sake," she said, her eyes troubled. Somehow she was always forgetting that.

"If you would just remember to do things in His name," said Andrew, anxious for her soul.

"But, Andy, I don't have time," she protested earnestly. "When somebody is dying you haven't time to think why you save them—you have to start doing it right away!"

But there was the world and all between these two and they looked at each other uncomprehendingly. Andrew was never without the thought of God in all he did. To Carie life was so nearly enough in its own richness.

Somewhere in this part of her life I must tell about Kuling. I think the telling belongs here after Wang Amah's illness, for Carie had said once more, "Every summer something terrible happens to us. If we could only get out of this dreadful heat of the Yangtse valley for a little while in the summer, the great fear of my life for the children would be gone."

Other white people scattered along the valley had the same fear for their children also, and an Englishman hunting in the Lu Mountains had found a spot for a summer refuge, a handful of lovely shallow valleys held on the top of a high mountain range. Here even in the middle of summer the air was sharp with chill at dawn and sunset and even at noon was invigorating with the coolness of mountain streams and mists. He spread the news of his find and a group of people joined to lease land on which to build tiny cottages of the stone abundant in the valleys.

Carie urged Andrew until he made a journey to see the spot, and he came back saying, "It is more like home than anything I have seen elsewhere in the world." It was enough. With what money they could muster, and I think for once Carie robbed Father's New Testament temporarily, they bought a bit of the land and the following summer Carie and the children took a steamer up the river to the town nearest the mountains and from there in a long day's ride by sedan chair they went through miles of rice fields and rolling bamboo-covered hills and at last began to ascend the mountain.

The air of the foothills was humid and depressing with the summer heat, but as the chair bearers began to swing up the mountain sides with sure-footed, rhythmic tread, a subtle sweet chill began to creep into the air and it filled Carie with excitement. This air had the very breath of the

West Virginia hills, and she had not smelled any like it since she had left her home. There were two hours of steady upward pull, the path a winding thread along the mountain side, and below were the rocky gorges over which the streams from the mountain tops poured in foaming, silvery falls or lay in deep green pools.

Such mountain flowers, too, she had never seen, not even in America. There the mountain flowers were small and scentless and exquisite. But here, brushing her chair as she passed them, bloomed great spotted red tiger lilies and tall white trumpet lilies streaked with purple on the back of their petals; here were long, delicate ferns, spraying everywhere, and under pine trees and feathery bamboo the earth was covered with thick and fern-like mosses. Here a vine threw a cascade of starry flowers over a tree, flowers rich in fragrance, and then, suddenly through the silence a deep, full, wild note called from some bird, loud and clear in its sweetness.

It was a beauty she had not dreamed possible in this country of crowded humanity, a country where she said always "there are too many living and too many dying." Lying back in her sedan chair she gazed up into the blue sky and saw with ecstasy the gathering of shining white mists over the peaks ahead and above her. Up and up they went until it seemed they would drive into the very sky itself, and then an unseen turn brought them into a narrow mountain pass, and there the mountain winds caught them, cold with the chill of mountain water and full of life and vigor.

The chair coolies put the chair down, then, and let the winds fly against their sweating, bare-back bodies, and then as for greeting, they sent out suddenly a strange, clear call that echoed and re-echoed among the peaks.

"Da la-la-la-la hoo-oo!"

Carie, hearing it, felt she might have shared in such a cry of delight herself, strange wild answer to the mountains.

Then came the final ascent into the valley, a swift short ascent, and there it lay like a bowl held high to the sky by the topmost peaks of the mountain range. At one side of the bowl was the little three-room stone cottage Andrew had had built.

None can measure what this cottage and the valley and the beauty and coolness meant to Carie then and in after years. The relief of coolness at night and of good sleep, the deep breathing of keen mountain air, the fresh cold water streaming out of a rock and fit for drinking without sterilizing, the freedom from anxiety of disease for two months, the joy of seeing the children grow rosy and round and chubby by the end of the summer when she had been wont to see them thin and pale and languid from sleepless nights and sore with prickly heat and boils —all this was inexpressible. Her thankfulness welled up in her and she would pray aloud sometimes with the children in one of those swift prayers of hers that were more like a beat from her heart than speech from her lips. These prayers she flung upward to God; whether He caught them or not she sent them up for sheer overflow of emotion.

She roamed the mountains with the children, picnicking here and there, anywhere. She was as fond as a child of eating out of doors and when Andrew was not there she might at any meal call gaily, "Let's pick up our plates and eat outside!"

There on the steps of the cottage or halfway up the hill as the mood caught them, they would sit and eat and watch the sun drop behind the mountain in the sudden way of mountain sunsets. But this only when Andrew was not there; he did not enjoy whimsy and sudden plans and the discomfort of a plate and no table, nor anything unusual, and when he was at home they must all sit decorously to grace and three meals, and Carie had to content herself with her chair placed so that she looked out of a door flung wide open.

For though Andrew came sometimes to the mountains for a brief holiday, he did not seem to mind the heat as she and the children did. He grew more lean, seemingly more imperturbably healthy as years passed. He did not, as she did, feel on his own flesh and spirit the sufferings of others. Music spoke to him not at all, and poetry never, and rarely even beauty in nature; the voice of human suffering, also, was too often for him the voice of those who cried out against the just punishments for their sins sent from a just God.

It was inevitable of course that this difference in the natures of husband and wife grew wider or at least more evident as time went on. Carie would not acknowledge even to herself their disunion, yet she showed it unconsciously in a thousand little impatiences which Andrew bore silently but visibly as a trial from God, and this manner of his endurance and even his extreme and quiet patience did not tend to make it easier for Carie, always uneasy because she felt she was not good enough and that after all he was "better" than she.

But this strain between the two did not appear much in the days when she had her children with her and dependent on her. Never was a woman more richly mother than this woman, bubbling over with a hundred little songs and scraps of gay nonsense to beguile a child from tears, and filled with wayward moods as she was, yet her hands were swift to tenderness and care and quiet brooding tending when need arose. Never was she more perfect mother than during the summers on the mountain top when she could give herself freely to her children. She led them here and there in search of beauty, and she taught them to love cliffs and rugged rocks outlined against the sky, and to love also little dells where ferns and moss grow about a pool. Beauty she brought into her house too and filled the rooms with ferns and flowers.

I think the search after God, which she never wholly gave up, was easier for her on this mountain top because God seemed more near where there was no human suffering to be seen. Almost any day there, she thought, where it was easy because of beauty to be patient and to be good, she might see Him. On Sunday mornings she went to church in the little stone church that was built

163

as the community grew, and it was part of the joy of the day that a clear little bell pealed out an invitation. I think she never heard it without thinking of her home, and when she went in answer to its call, she went half in memory of her home across the sea. But partly, too, she went to worship and to sing, even to worship that which she did not understand. For this woman, this American woman, was so built by blood and training that all her joys led her in spite of herself to something higher than she thought herself, so that she must go seeking in spirit for that someone—that something to praise and thank when life seemed good to her. She was one whom happiness and peace moved to the very best effort in her, and suffering and too much pain drove her mad and defiant.

Thus swiftly here and slowly there nine years passed and again they were free if they wished to take a furlough for a year and go home. They made ready to go one June, letting the cottage in the mountains to friends who needed it and setting sail from the coast to cross the Pacific Ocean. During these years Edwin had grown to manhood, interminable years when measured by her constant thoughts of him and by her fears and sleepless nights. He had finished college and was now ready for the university, and they were therefore to spend most of this year in America, not at the big white house but in the university town where Edwin was to be, the same university his father had attended. This university was in the little old Virginia town of Lexington, filled with historic meaning and atmosphere, and Carie looked forward to this eagerly, thinking that here she could steep the younger children in the feeling for their own country, which not having seen they yet loved.

But first there was the sea to cross and she was ill and wretched as ever so that when San Francisco drew near she could not set foot upon the beloved soil fast enough. She pointed out this and that to the two little girls who stared at everything, enormous eyed, proud beyond measure of the astounding magic of running water and of electric lights and of the stateliness of tall buildings. Was it not all America, and was not America theirs?

One thing only shocked them. It was to see white men loading trucks and handling baggage.

"Mother," asked Comfort in horror, "are even the coolies over here white people?"

Carie laughed. "We don't have coolies in our country," she answered. "That is why people are happy. Everybody works and it's no disgrace to work with your hands."

But such questions always sobered her lest these children in spite of her be marked by the Orient. She was troubled now and resolved that in this very year Comfort should learn how to cook and sew and wash dishes and to perform all the womanly round. She was a great believer in housework as a cure for women's discontents.

"Every woman ought to know how to keep house and make bread and cook and sew," she declared. "It doesn't matter how many servants you have you ought to know how to do these things if you are a woman." And afterwards to Comfort, who was at times a bit sulky over the practice of this theory, she said, "Some time in your life you will have to do it for yourself. Besides, we Americans *work!*"

It was the final word, the tradition of her race to be upheld by her hands. And indeed in that fearless, vigorous body of hers there was not one drop of languorous blood.

The railway journey across the United States was always a joy and a possession to Carie. To see her country unroll itself before her eyes, to see the beauty of mountain and field and plain, to watch lamps lit in little houses at evening, to enter into the life of streets and villages and cities was like music to her, and she sat by the car window watching the pageant pass, her eyes brilliant. Every slightest growth and change she noted, every sign of prosperity she rejoiced in, pointing them out to her children.

But this time America held a special meaning for her.
There was Edwin, a grown man.

Here was the home town again, here the white gate,
the great maple, the big house that was forever home.
There was her father, slight, still straight as a youth,
white-haired, fastidious in his spotless linen and black
suit—was Hermanus never to grow too old for vanity?
—this other white-haired figure, could this be Cornelius
grown so old and bent?—these young women his daughters, this young man his son, a big square-shouldered boy,
ruddy-cheeked, here his young wife grown settled and
matronly? Nine years indeed had passed. When she
looked in the mirror of her old room there above her
temples were the two white wings of her own hair and
the deep bloom was gone from her cheeks.

Each sister had gone now to her own home and the
house seemed strange without them there to meet her at
the door. But there, but there, shy in the offing, was a
tall, slender thoughtful-looking young man. It was Edwin. When Carie would have put her arms about her son's
neck he was grown so tall he must stoop so that she could
clasp her hands behind his head. He wore pince-nez and
a high collar and looked far more than his twenty-one
years. She held him off, at arm's length, to see him thoroughly. It was a good gaze that met hers, a little dreaming, perhaps, but gentle and true and intelligent. What
lay behind those grave, short-sighted eyes she must find
out anew, for it was plain her little boy was gone.

Then it was a delight to her to take her two little girls
and lead them all over the farm and village, pointing
out every remembered place, meeting every old friend.
Here in this quiet place of homes was for her the very
heart of America. On Sunday there was the renewal of
joy to go again to church, and to hear the little, sharp,
sweet church bell whose tones she never forgot. Hermanus, now very old, still marshalled the family as before,
and marched at their head down the village street, the
whole family filing behind. Now she and Andrew and
their three children were part of the beloved ritual. In

the church Andrew's brother still preached, white-haired and very frail in these days. He had never wholly recovered from the hardships of the Civil War and an old wound broke out again and again in his hip. But he managed still to preach his gentle, unworldly, doctrinal sermons, and it was food to Carie's soul to hear his voice once more.

America, America, how could she ever leave it again!

After the happy summer, when she had delighted in all the old tasks of churning and washing under the trees and ironing in the cool buttery, of canning the rich harvest of fruits, after a round of visits to her married sisters and brother—was it possible that little Greta was this dark-eyed mother of children, all her mischief subdued but not gone, and this Luther, this settled prosperous merchant, now the father of four children?—they went to Lexington and found a rambling old house on the edge of the town, furnished after a fashion, and there she had her first home in America. It was an old house belonging to the period before the Civil War, and the kitchen was far from the house in the rooms that had been connected with the slave quarters, and she had to pass back and forth through a tangle of garden. To another it might have seemed too tiresome, but to her it was a privilege to look over the garden to the hillside rising beyond and a wood. She made her work light with her swift step and her ready songs, and the work seemed nothing after the life she had had. She had only her own family to look after, only to feed and tend and amuse them. There were none of the other demands made upon her that she had had in China, demands of sickness and sadness and human need. This lifting of the burden of sympathy for a brief space was in itself rest to her.

Nor did she have to teach her children, for Comfort could go to school for the year, Edwin was in the university delighting her with his brilliant scholarship, and Faith was at her skirts for a playmate. It was a time for reunion. In the evening they gathered about the old stone hearth and Andrew made a fire of logs and for their supper they drank milk, "from a cow" Faith explained with gravity every evening, and ate great gingerbread cookies and the fruits they could not eat in China.

At such times as these Carie watched her son and tried to find out what he was and to establish again the old close tie that had bound them together before he left her. She longed passionately for him to become all that she was not. But she found his very gentleness evasive. He seemed yielding, candid, and certainly he was kind, and yet she felt him far from her. In the end, against her will, she let him be, and waited, sorely conscious of separation from him, whom somehow she had thought she would still find her little boy. But during these years alone, the man had come into being, and he could not again be dependent on her.

Perhaps this independence made it easier for her at the end of the year to turn back again to the Orient where there were many who needed her still. Twenty-two years now she had been away from this country of hers. She held it fast in her heart as she ever had, ever it was the fairest and best of lands, God-blessed. But the niche in it that had been hers was closing now. Twenty years, and her brothers and sisters had learned to live without her, although they loved her well. Twenty years, and the daughters of Cornelius were young women in the room where she had lived as a young woman; their dresses, long skirts, and full leg-o-mutton sleeves hung where her crinolines had hung, and their snapshots of boarding school days were caught in a fish-net, as the fad was, on the wall where the little dark madonna had been when she was young. In the room where her mother had died, Cornelius had lived so many years with his wife that even Hermanus seemed to have forgotten the wife who had loved him so ardently. In the village old Mr. and Mrs. Dunlop were long dead, her school friends were married and gone, and only old Neale Carter, still a bachelor, lived drowsy and alone with his negroes. The sight of him, huge and red and blustering between fits of drowsiness, ended forever the romance that might have been. He had forgotten everything except his food and his juleps.

Yes, she had left America, and America had forgotten her, and were she to come back to it permanently she must build herself anew into another niche.

But there could be no question of that, for long before the year was out Andrew was impatient to be at his work again. His own old home had been sold, his parents were dead, and now his whole heart lay among the dark people. Moreover, America, he felt, had no need of him. There were preachers and churches everywhere, and all who would could "hear and be saved." Those in the far land who could not hear if they would, for there was no one to tell them, called to him so he heard nothing else, and the next summer when Edwin had finished his university work with honors and had found the principalship of a school and was indeed wholly independent, they prepared to go back.

There was a deep sadness in Carie's heart when she came to say farewell to her son this time. Somehow if America held him, and she would have America hold her son, then she herself had lost him, although she scarcely knew how. Yet he was a man now and must choose his own life, and was she to blame him if he chose his own country when she had taught him from his birth to love his country well? But in choosing it meant that she, his mother, must live now in exile from her son, seeing him perhaps only once or twice more while she lived. She left America with rare tears brimming in her eyes and loneliness in her heart. There was more than the physical separation this time; there was the beginning of a separation of the spirit, and she went out somehow homeless.

Once more then, she went back to the river port to the bungalow set in the circle of hills above the dark Chinese city lying like lees along the river's edge. She set herself now in that quietness of spirit, which was the nearest that her exuberant nature ever came to despondency, to the making of her home and her garden again. Signs of her age were upon her. Her hair grew white, although it kept its curly thickness and softness and remained a crown of beauty to her always. The mature curves of her middle life changed to slightness again.

I think she felt at this time of her life that she had parted entirely from her girlhood except as it was a memory with her. America had grown on beyond her, forgotten her, filled her place. One must grow with a country, grow within it, if one is to belong to it wholly. Therefore she was glad she had given her son to America. As for her, for the first time in her life she set herself seriously to her own life, not realizing that she was America, that she brought America with her wherever she was, to all whom she met.

Once again she took up her work of friendship to the people about her. Once again she set herself to shape the environment she wished for her own children. Comfort was a tall girl now, a difficult child in many ways, wilful, passionate—if Carie had been able to see it, much like herself. But Carie could only see with a sort of fear and sorrow that this child of hers was so built that she must suffer in life as her mother had through too sensitive a nature and too much emotion, and Carie tried to teach her daughter self-control, Carie, whose own battle had never been completely won with herself! But she planned tasks for the girl's day, taught her music and painting, saw to it that every week there was a long composition written that she might learn how to write well. For both of the children Carie did all that she could and quite alone, with one of the aids that modern mothers have. Their bodies she trained and made supple through exercise, correcting their posture, encouraging them to every sort of physical bravery.

I remember that she offered a silver coin for every crow's nest that Comfort could bring down. The crows built high in the tops of the trees, and one of the sensations this girl, now a middle-aged woman, will never forget is that of climbing higher and higher, on a windy March day, higher and higher up a wind-tossed, slender tree trunk, and reaching at last the nest. One had to climb early, for once the nest was built Carie's softness of heart would not allow her to see it destroyed. But what she wanted the child to learn was to dare to take physical risks.

I was not always easy, however, to make Comfort submit to the daily routine. She could resist mightily and with gusto, and at last Carie saw that if she was to win it must be by approval and stimulation of ambition, for the girl would not be driven. Carie learned from that quick sympathy of hers to look at last into her own heart and see what would win the child's and thus the wayward adolescent period passed more easily for them both. But in spite of passionate mother and passionate daughter Carie shaped well her child's environment and filled her life with what was the best in the culture of her own country and set her feet firmly and forever on the path of desire for what was beautiful and good. It was no mean achievement since except for books and natural beauty there was no other aid.

Beyond this life for her children, Carie's days were filled as never before with the people about her. This came about especially after one of the much dreaded famine years. A fearful year was the year of 1905, when crops failed so that even in the rich Yangtse valley, so fertile and well drained, food was short, and this especially when refugees began to pour down from the north.

As winter started the city and countryside began to be filled with the wretched creatures, men, women, and children, who came on foot, begging as they came for food to keep them alive, and dying all along the way. Cold weather came on and still they arrived in increasing numbers, haggard, grim, dropping in death. Carie, who had seen her fill of sad sights, was moved to new agony and the utmost of pity, and she exerted all her powers to give what she had and to collect money here and there. There were no desserts on her table that year, and every scrap she could save was saved. Even the New Testament had to wait that year.

She dared not go by day to give the scant relief at her disposal, so inadequate was it to the need, for to the gathered thousands of starving people it was nothing, and her life was endangered by the giving of it, lest they fall upon her and fight for what she had. She went about empty-handed among the huts during the day, therefore, and noted the worst cases, and at night she put on Wang Amah's old coat and with Wang Amah beside her she crept among the people, leaving a dollar here and a bundle of food there.

Andrew was away from home that entire winter. He was in the north where the famine was worst, administering relief from the sums of money sent from America. From these sums he sent a little to Carie, to whom the money was the more precious because it came from the plenty and the ready generous hearts of her own people.

"It is from America, for you—from America!"

Over and over again I have heard her say these words. She became to those hopeless folk a living embodiment of America.

Sometimes it was not money but shiploads of food that came from America, and the food was not always suitable. I remember one ship brought hundreds of slightly damaged cheeses. Almost the only food these people could not eat was cheese, an article apparently nauseous to Chinese universally except as they acquire the taste for it abroad. Carie looked with tragic eyes on all the cheeses dumped on the quay at the river's edge, and then promptly became a cheese monger. She went to every white man's house and with her ready tongue and warm heart persuaded the white community, not large at best, to purchase the outrageous numbers of cheeses. She herself stocked her cellars with them, buying all she could not sell, and we had those "famine cheeses" for years to come. But with the money she bought rice and flour in great triumph and fed many refugees.

But the grievous sights she now saw daily and hourly

wore on her spirit until it seemed she would break under the strain of her sadness and her impotence, in spite of all, to do more that only a little in proportion to the need. She had not believed, even she, that such misery was possible to flesh, such slow torture of swollen shapes of death, such dreary, hopeless-eyed little children, such fierce wild selfishness for food, even sometimes between mother and child, often between husband and wife.

It became impossible at last to hide her identity from the people in the huts and they traced her to her home, and crazed with hunger they staggered up the hill to the bungalow and beat upon the gates of the compound and lay in dreadful, shivering hordes against the walls. I think not one suffered as Carie did then. Her food was ashes in her mouth and she could scarcely eat because of those who had nothing. Yet she did not dare let them in for fear they would devour everything and in their great numbers be no better off than they were before.

But the sound of the moaning and the calling aloud of her name through day and night, the dead that lay there at each dawn to be carried away, drove her nearly mad with helpless pity and angry sorrow. All the old fierce anger against a God who could let this be swelled up once more in her heart. But she had been taught that she must not question God. He knew best. All was in His will. Her struggle to believe in her old creed, "Trust and obey," and her torn heart were pitiful to see. She set herself with desperate determination to do all she could, and devoted herself to the finding of food, night and day, going into the houses of the rich, going everywhere as she would never have done on any other errand than human need.

She no longer tried to shield her children; indeed, she could not. What wall could shut out this wailing of the people, these last cries of failing hope, the saddest of all the weak voices of little children? No, they must see what life could do. She pressed them into her service, being careful only to keep them from extreme sights of painful death.

There was no Christmas that year. Every year of her

life she had made Christmas the happiest, merriest time for her children. The trimming of the house with holly and greens, and the stirring of the plum pudding had always been rites in the family life. Here as elsewhere she had had to provide all, for there were no toy shops, no Christmas display, to help her. But she could make Christmas a very orgy of gingerbread men and ladies and toys she manufactured, of things both useful and nonsensical, of stockings hung at the hearth on Christmas Eve, and on Christmas morning a tree trimmed with what she had made of bits of bright paper and ribbon she had saved throughout the year. It was one time in the year when she gave herself wholeheartedly to gayety, and nothing was allowed to spoil the pleasure of the season and to shatter the sweet mystery of Christmas Eve and the Manger Story told about an open fire and carols sung at the organ before bedtime. In the morning her brilliant voice rang through the house at dawn, "Joy to the World, the Lord Is Come!"

So she created Christmas for her children. So she built into them the tradition and deep meaning of Christmas so that they never forgot it and to this day, scattered over three continents as they are and she buried in a fourth beneath alien soil, Christmas stirs them with profoundest memories. Yet she took pains always to make them realize that it was a time of sharing and each child was taught to prepare gifts not only for parents and each other but for servants and little Chinese friends and any whom they knew to be in special need, also. Well she knew the pleasure of sharing and the good content that follows it.

But on this year's Christmas she had no heart to make merry, even for her children. How could one rejoice, how make plum pudding and stir fruit cakes when outside the walls there were those?

"Children, we can't have Christmas this year," she said soberly. "Let's take all we would have spent and all we can spare besides and buy food for these others."

It was a strange Christmas day, spent in cooking great vats of rice and distributing it bowl by bowl through a crack in the gate until none was left and we had done all we could. It was a long, silent day. She could not even sing at evening. As reward there was less weeping in the night and she slept a little more.

Of all this Faith was mercifully too little to grasp the full significance but upon Comfort it made an impression too deep for her years. As spring wore on somehow and the ones who were left from the winter's death gathered themselves together and took their way home again in the hope of planting their land, the young girl was nervous and distraught and Carie saw that she must go away for a little while. There was a boarding school in Shanghai kept by some New England women and here Carie decided to send the girl for the two years that yet remained before she was old enough to go back to America for college.

Comfort had, indeed, been too much alone and was overgiven to dreaming. The loneliness of a child growing up in an alien land was weighing too heavily upon her and so Carie prepared to send her away.

It seemed to Carie that she was never to have any comfort in her children. This country—this work—demanded them sacrificed, if not in death at least in separation. But this sadness she kept much in her heart, striving to make the separation seem for Comfort only a happy going away to find friends of her own age and kind. She took great pains to prepare a dainty wardrobe of simple clothes and packed them with care in the round-backed trunk that had gone so many times already over land and sea, and Andrew took Comfort to school. Then there was only little Faith left in the house, a serious, quiet little girl.

The strain of the winter was somewhat wiped away by another of the blessed summers in the little mountain cottage. Other white people, an increasing number, gathered there now, and there was for Carie not only the physical renewal from air and sky and mountains, but the renewal of friendship with people of her own kind and culture. This she rejoiced in. It meant much to be able to escape even for a few weeks the pulling of her heart that she could not avoid as she came and went among the Chinese women.

It was well for her to withdraw sometimes into a place where she could steep herself in peace and beauty as she could in the mountain valley, and this summer she spent in her garden, planting ferns here and wild flowers there and pruning trees and shrubs that grew wild about the place. It was the best way in which she could restore her soul.

All these years Andrew had been going steadily about the countryside on foot or on a small grey ass, until by now he had churches in many villages, and church members proud enough to feel themselves demeaned by a pastor who rode a donkey. He came home one day riding upon a plump white pony which his parishioners had given him, and to Carie's astonished question he replied embarrassed and yet pleased, "I oughtn't to have it, perhaps—our Lord rode upon an ass."

But Carie had fallen in love with the horse and was patting its black nose. She said quickly, "I daresay He would have ridden a horse if anyone had given Him one."

At this time of her life, with only one child left in her home, Carie returned to her work in the churches with Andrew, and made great plans for the Chinese women. She went with Andrew often and they bought a small junk and went through the winding canals to towns and villages, Faith with them. Between teaching Faith her lessons and keeping tidy house on the junk Carie taught women and girls.

She and Andrew had hot arguments sometimes over the conflict of Christian doctrine and circumstances they found. For instance there was Mr. Ling who wanted to join the church but who had two wives. To Andrew the only possible solution was to bid him send his concubine away. But Carie listened to the concubine and knew her despair and she argued with Andrew, "But the poor woman has nowhere to go—it's not *her* fault!"

Then Andrew's ministerial right grew strong. He would not let his sense of the principle be weakened.

"Mr. Ling will have to stay out of the church, then," he said firmly.

"It's cruel!" cried Carie with all her old heat against injustice. "If it's God Himself I'll still say it's cruel!"

To this Andrew would give no answer. There were other difficulties, too. Carie discovered that a pastor in whom Andrew trusted was smoking opium. She had suspected him for a long time, having an extraordinary intuition about people. But Andrew would hear nothing against him. One day she saw a paper drop out of the man's Bible. Before he could pick it up Carie had it. It was a bill for opium.

Another time she heard a whisper against another trusted assistant of Andrew's, and again she found proof that he was charging an admission fee to all who entered the church. There were times when it paid people to become church members, for "foreigners" were powerful and they shared the protection of their treaties with all who called themselves Christians, and the churches were crowded. Andrew would not have been human if he had found Carie's sharpness altogether pleasing, and certainly he was not happier because she was right.

But Carie could work in no other way. She must know the truth. To the woman, pouring out her story of her troubles as a concubine, she listened and said quickly, "Of course I see exactly how it is. What can we do about it?"

And she sent up one of her swift, half-conversational prayers, "God, You see this woman. You understand the difficulty she is in. She can't help it. If we can't think of a way out, we'll have to take her as she is."

Afterwards she was smitten with fear lest she had done wrong and answered her own heart, saying, "Well, if I can understand I should think God could."

But she was never quite sure. There was Andrew. Perhaps God was like Andrew.

Carie's home in these years became increasingly the gathering place for all kinds of people in trouble. There was something about her cheery, comfortable way, her gay, bright voice, her love of sunshine and flowers and happy-looking rooms, her sparkling eyes, her sane, good presence that somehow set things on the way to righting themselves. In these days there came often into her living room a tall, handsome woman, black-haired, black-eyed, with a smooth, pale olive skin, always beautifully gowned in Paris gowns. She was the daughter of a British business man of means in the port, a man of education and high in office.

In his youth this man, like many others, had taken into his house a Chinese woman, an ignorant, pretty girl with whom he had become infatuated in a sing-song house, and by her he had two children, a boy and a girl. The son was a dissipated scoundrel, continually drunk, but when there was condemnation of him and his father had rescued him once more from one of his incessant scrapes, Carie always said, "Poor Harry Evans—he is so lonely. No one will have him, white or Chinese. He has no country—that's the loneliest thing on earth."

But if the son was lonely, the daughter Ella, a beautiful, proud creature, was lonely beyond imagination. She took the place of mistress in her father's house, for the Chinese woman as she grew older degenerated into the commonest of her class and never appeared in public. The white father, however, was pathetically proud of the daughter's stately beauty and calm dignity, and she sat at the foot of the table and was the hostess of his elaborate dinner parties. Chinese men were never tolerated in that house except as menials and she had no opportunity, therefore, of meeting Chinese gentlemen, who would doubtless have despised her. But indeed she was English, and Chinese in nothing except the pointed beauty of her hands and in the duskiness of her coloring. Yet these slight traces made it impossible in those times for an Englishman to consider her as his wife, and so she lived on in the house, English and not English, of the white people and yet eternally alien.

This woman had her hours of utter despair and these she learned to conceal from her father, for the old man truly loved her and could not forgive himself for the wrong he felt he had done her in pouring this mixture of blood into her veins, and when he saw her in her dark moods he could not be comforted and regretted bitterly the folly he had committed in allowing his fancy for a pretty face and the clamor of his flesh to condemn this proud daughter to life.

Then Ella Evans found Carie and it is thus I remember her, coming to the gate at evening usually in the falling dusk, in her handsome sedan chair, and then sitting in the twilit living room waiting until Carie was free to talk. What the two talked about I do not know, for Carie always shut the door and I could hear only their murmuring voices. But once when they came out I saw Miss Evans bend over Carie from her height and gaze earnestly and speechlessly into Carie's clear, straight-gazing eyes, and that night at the supper table Carie was a little silent and unwontedly sad.

Sometimes the waiting one would be a small, kimono-clad figure. That was the Japanese wife of the strange old Englishman who lived in a wooden house built Japanese fashion in a hollow of the distant hills. There was a tale in the port about this old man, white-haired and frail with age when I knew him, but very erect still and courteous and very much the reserved and independent English gentleman. He had had a post, it was said, in the customs at this same port in the early days and he was the younger son of an English baronet, sent out to seek his fortune, as so many are sent in like circumstances to the Orient. There was a girl in England whom he loved and she was to come out to him as soon as he had his first promotion, a fluffy, yellow-haired child, the story went, and when he had worked for three endless years he sent for her, for he had enough to make a fit home for her.

There were the wildest tales of the house he made for

her and the things he bought for it in Shanghai—Aubusson carpets and satin-covered furniture and a rosewood piano, things he had starved himself to buy and gone in debt for besides. He went to the coast to meet her, burning under that cool exterior of his. When the ship came in there was only a note for him.

"I am so sorry, dear Ronald, but it was all a mistake. "I don't—I can't love you."

She had run away with the ship's purser. Ronald Stearns folded the note very small and tore it into bits and dropped it into the curling, muddy waters of the Whangpoo, and that night he went into a Japanese brothel of the better sort and bought a woman for himself, a conscientious, polite, cleanly little woman, somewhat older than the others and not at all pretty.

He made a great ceremony of asking her in marriage and took her to the British Consulate, she very much bewildered with the turn in her fortunes, and paddling anxiously down the corridors behind him in her *geta*. There, in spite of the remonstrances of the British consul, Ronald Stearns married the little Japanese and took her back to the port.

He built her a Japanese house on the hillside, too far for visitors, and he sold at auction the rosewood piano and the Aubusson carpets and the satin-covered furniture and all the trinkets he had accumulated. When I knew him he had lived for many years in great dignity and respectability, but he never took any part in the narrow social life of the white people at the port and his intercourse with them was limited strictly to business. When his father died he fell heir to some fortune, but he never went back to England, and lived on with his Japanese wife, to whom he was always the figure of kindness and courtesy. They were childless.

Why little Mrs. Stearns came to see Carie I do not know. Perhaps only for a friendly talk with a woman, for this was the loneliest possible little creature, gay as she was in her flowered silk kimonos and richly hued sashes. She spoke very little English and this was significant of her companionship with her English husband. But by every circumstance her life must have been far from his. He read much and after business hours spent much time in study, although he was always punctilious in walking with her of an evening in the pretty Japanese garden he had had made for her. It was silent walking, for there was little to be said between them. All his world of breeding and experience she could not dream of and her small life was so simple that it was a primer to him. Yet Carie could fill some need for companionship in this life.

But there were more than a few among the white people of the port who turned to her. There was the poor crazed Englishwoman who used to come through the night in her sedan, the passionate, jealous wife of a cold and cruel husband. Into Carie's ear she poured without reserve the tragedy of her life, and after she had gone Carie's eyes were sick with some horror of too much knowledge, knowledge she fain would not have had.

There was the thin, consumptive Scotchwoman, who had once been a missionary and who married a whiskey-drinking Scotch captain of a river steamer to reform him and saw him after the honeymoon take to his drink again. All her desperate little efforts at amusing him, of holding his love to a pitch where it might strengthen his will, all the futile attempts of a woman not handsome enough, not charming enough, to hold any man—these she poured out to Carie, coughing and weeping.

"If I could only have a child," she used to moan. "He wants a little daughter."

But that thin, bent body of hers could bear no such fruit and at last she adopted a child from an orphanage in Australia and they made another start together. But in less than a year the child caught smallpox from a Chinese servant and died, and the father, who had learned to love the little yellow-haired thing, became a drunkard in earnest and poor Mrs. Gibbs died of the disease she had had for so long.

These and many others of those who drift through the ports of the Orient came into Carie's home and received from her the succor of her wholesome personality. There seemed, indeed, always someone waiting for her. Even the half-breed Indian doctor and his dark, stout wife found in her a special friend, although she could never see them without a pang of memory for the sweet son she had lost.

At this time of her life Carie was an extraordinarily attractive and magnetic person. Some of the impetuosity of her youth had passed out of her, taking with it a heat of temper at times too swift for comfort. She was mellowed in sympathy, yet so vigorous that she brought with her always a breeze of vital, genial American womanhood. In her presence one thought of the good and simple things of life. She was so normal, so full of a keen humor, so sane in an atmosphere where too often white men and women become changed and saddened and subtly degraded. She was always robustly herself.

In her home she had created the very atmosphere of her own nature. She had always a good vegetable garden, a thrifty-looking American garden, and on her table one ate lima beans and tomatoes and asparagus and Irish potatoes and lettuce, all the good American foods that seemed somehow in those days never to be found elsewhere. She could not tolerate the stringiness of the roaming half-wild Chinese fowl, and she had always a small chicken run and fresh eggs and a fat hen ready for roasting or in the spring young frying chickens that she prepared in the most delectable southern style. Biscuits came from her hands light as cloudlets and her coconut cakes and black chocolate cakes and fruit cakes and marble loaf cakes were enough to woo a man a hundred miles to find them. I remember her often in her busiest days kneading great masses of light, snowy bread dough, and afterwards turning out of the pans the big sweet loaves and the whole house was full of the good fragrance.

By such wholesome and simple ways she healed those who came to her, and in the way she had, by being only herself and what she was, she brought home and country to the exiled.

I think these years that merged into the last third of her life were happy ones. She had learned now that home and country are in one's own heart, and may be created according to that heart's desire anywhere in the world. The old sick longing for the West Virginia hills and the old sweet life passed. These were her possessions forever in memory, and could not be taken from her; indeed, they were only in memory, for change had laid hold on what had been her own. Hermanus, her father, died at a great age, fastidious to the end, and death scarcely separated her more than life had from him. His memory took its place in her mind beside other memories that would be living to her as long as she lived and she did not grieve.

True to her determination, she moved her home no more. North and south and east and west Andrew traveled during these years, but he went alone, coming back from time to time for refreshment to the restful home she made for them all. It was what was best for him, too, for he was not a man fitted to family cares, and spared now the trouble and vexation of spirit of moving about with the belongings of a family, he went pioneering where his contented spirit called, and it was the voice of God to him.

As for Carie, she could plant a tree and hope for fruitage and her roses climbed to the roof of the bungalow, and no more did she have to drag her children from one wretched hovel to another. There in the bungalow she built their environment. There were picnics to the hills and to bamboo-circled temples. Did ever anyone look more alien in a Buddhist temple than she, I wonder, standing sturdy and practical and unmoved before the sinister Oriental gods? It stands in my memory as one of the fantastic contrasts of my experience. In a court where a thousand years had left its greyness she dispensed sandwiches and cocoa briskly and fed her flock, and if she looked at the silent gods it was as a strong modern spirit views the myths of the dead.

Every little talent her children had, she nurtured carefully. Not only were there picnics and long walks and the studying of botany and plant life by such pleasant ways, but she devised little social occasions of one sort or another whereby they might learn to conduct themselves gracefully so that when they went out of this somewhat limited life they would not be at a loss. One of the most special occasions were little quarterly musicales she gave, when she not only sang most beautifully herself, but saw to it that each of her children contributed something. She had them print out the simple programs and paint designs on them to enhance their appearance and all this for the sake of her children, that their lives might lack nothing to train them for life anywhere in the world.

These years were a time of unprecedented peace in China. The retribution that had fallen upon the country after the attempt to expel the foreigner in the Boxer Rebellion had left the people stricken with a sense of their own weakness and the power of the foreigner for a few brief years was strong as it was not before and has not been since. The white man then was safe to come and go as he would everywhere, for behind every foreigner the Chinese saw warships and deadly guns and swift and ruthless soldiery. This made for temporary peace, at least.

Best of all for Carie, there were no more deaths in her house. She could find comfort in the developing lives of her children and feel safe. Edwin was married now, and although she had not seen his wife and the first grandchild that was hers, she was glad that there was someone to take her place with her son and make a home for him and see to all the thousand little deeds that make a man happy and comfortable. Comfort also was growing and while the relationship between mother and daughter at this time of the girl's adolescence was such that Carie was often sorely tried, yet she was proud of the child. It was fast nearing the time when this one, too, must be sent to America.

As for small Faith, this child was of all her children, except perhaps Clyde, the one most dear to Carie. In appearance she was like Clyde, with the same loosely curling dark hair and the big, dark blue eyes, true violet eyes. In nature she was more suited to her mother than was Comfort. She was a tender-hearted, sympathetic, amenable child, even-tempered and companionable. Comfort had inherited her mother's faults too closely, a swift, wilful temper, a sensuous love of beauty and music; all those parts of her own nature which Carie struggled most heartily to overcome she saw to her dismay born again in this tall wilful daughter of hers. But Faith was more like Andrew, less impetuous, more easily self-controlled, quiet and of lesser speech; and more than she realized at the time, more indeed than was good for the child's serious, sensitive nature, Carie made of her a confidante and friend.

These were, moreover, the years of Carie's greatest physical vitality. She was past the age of child-bearing and had no longer upon her the strain of little children. The hill climate above the river port suited her well and she was stronger than she had ever been in the flat lands of the upper Grand Canal. She was busy also, and had found her place in the mixed community of overwhelming Chinese life and the fringe upon its edge, mingling slightly, of white women and men.

But deep down under all the fullness of her life, Carie felt at times still the inadequacy of her relation to God. She planned sometimes for a period when she would withdraw and really seek to find what she needed. She planned to read her Bible more and to pray more and try to be "good." She never understood her own nature well enough to know that when she took time to withdraw from human life and from men and women and all their human needs, it would be only because she was dead. Life was a stronger challenge, after all, than the hereafter and she could never resist a challenge. She liked to feel her brain and resourcefulness put to the test. She was, to give a small instance, no great lover of games, because there were too many other things she wanted to do, but she loved chess, and this, I think, only because it challenged her brains.

I remember she used often to look somewhat ruefully at her hands, those beautiful, useful, roughened hands of hers, so strong in the palm, so unexpectedly delicate and pointed in the fingers; not small hands, but having spare and well-shaped lines. It was always her plan that one day she would stop plunging her hands into this and that; she was going to wear gloves when she gardened and use cold cream and have really "nice" hands. She loved the white hands of ladies, the skin soft and smooth and the nails pink and tapering. But if she ever remembered to put on gloves, as sometimes once in a long time she did, sooner or later they would be off and she would be grubbing about in the earth, looking up to say apologetically, "I seem to have to feel the roots are right. They won't grow otherwise. And I do like the feel of the earth!"

We who knew her would only laugh and tease her for her vanity, for well we knew those hands of hers would go into everything, from gardening to washing some child's sore skin.

"Well, when I am old, then, and when I can't work—" she would maintain, laughing herself.

Ah, that old age of hers that never came, the time when she was going to do all sorts of things from making her hands nice and being a dignified old lady—she dignified, who at any moment could be overcome with mirth! —to reading her Bible more and finding out about God —the old age that never came, and never could come to one so incurably vivid and young as she!

How can I give a true picture of her life, bound as it was by the necessity for the most rigid economy so that every newspaper even was saved for what its use might be in the house, economy that might have crushed a spirit less stout! My memory of her is of someone always marvelously fresh and pretty, although when I examine it I see that she wore the same dresses year after year. But she could twist a ribbon in such a way or so pin a flower at her throat that she looked as though she wore a new gown. There was that air about her. I remember that she had a large old tin box in the attic where she put every hat, I believe, she ever owned, when it grew past use, and every flower of silk or bit of ribbon. Twice a year she cried gaily, "We must go to Paris to buy our hats for the season!"

And with great ceremony we went to the attic and opened the tin box and out of it by means of her skilful fingers hats were made for herself and the two girls. Nor do I remember any sense of discontent with what she fashioned. If anything her hats were prettier than any I saw elsewhere, and had style. She might have been, if she had not been what she was, a first-rate milliner, or a singer or an artist or any one of the other things she could have been. At any rate, her imagination and gay nonsense and swift fingers created for us all the illusion and excitement of shopping for a new hat. Years later when I really did go to Paris to buy a new hat there was not half the edge of excitement in it that there had been in the old expeditions up the attic stairs to Paris in a tin box.

Seven years passed thus, more swiftly than any other seven years of her life. Good years they were when death did not once come to her house. She grew deeper and deeper in human wisdom and was withal the richest and most beautiful nature, although she never lost her faults. In spite of moments of friction her children thought of her as boon companion and best of fun, although these times of fun were perhaps less frequent than they had been. She grew in patience and in understanding, although she was never a creature of patience when her indignation was stirred.

Then the time came once more for her return to America for a year of furlough. Comfort was now a slender young woman of seventeen, and ready for college; an eager, shy, childish creature, full of contradictions and in many ways strangely mature. Carie felt she wanted to give her some parting gift at this time of oncoming separation, something to satisfy the child's love of beauty and adventure. After some thought she decided that this gift would be to return to America through Europe. She wanted to share with the children the memories she still had of other countries.

I think about this time came the great battle of Father's New Testament, and the only time when Carie succeeded, by dint of great determination and some temper, in making Andrew postpone a long-planned new edition, so that Comfort could have some new clothes for college. At any rate, the girl heard carefully muted but violent arguments behind the closed door of her parents' bedroom, and she remembers her father coming out thoughtful and not a little dejected, and her mother, determined and flushed and very bright-eyed, and saying, "I am going to get you that other dress, after all, child, and we are going home by Europe."

This time they took the railway journey through Siberia that Carie might be spared the sea. They went by steamer up the Yangtse and then at Hankow took rail for the north. Caire was as vividly interested in everything new as the children. In Russia particularly she was absorbed. She saw here the essentials of a grave and dangerous human situation and was appalled by the differences between the few rich and educated and the millions of common people, living in a manner almost bestial. She kept saying, "These people are going to make a revolution one day that will shake the world. You can't have this sort of thing in a country and be safe."

In less than ten years her prediction had come true and at that time she watched the world shake as she had said it would, and followed with keenest interest the steps in the Russian revolution, her sympathy with the people in spite of her native conservatism that hated excesses.

But through this summer they took their fill of the

beautiful places in Europe, each seeing what he liked most. Andrew's interest was in churches and cathedrals, and Comfort was a glutton for everything. But Carie delighted most in homes and farms and in people. They spent two months on the edge of a blue lake in Switzerland in a little château kept open for tourists by the widow of a man who had once lived there rich and had died poor. Carie divided her interest between the beauty of lake and snowy Alps and the tales of the little widow. There was always someone telling her story to Carie. The very chambermaids in the hotels were confiding in her by the end of the second day of her stay anywhere.

When the time came to turn to America the old eagerness did not fall upon Carie as it had before. I think she approached her country even dubiously. America was fast in her heart. Would the reality be as she saw it there? Last time she had not been sure of her place—life had gone on yet seven more years without her. What would it be this time? She heard many new things. People said the country was full of new inventions, automobiles for instance, strange machinery to keep house with. It was all very different.

But if America were strange, there was Edwin to be seen, and his wife and the little grandchild. These were enough for eager anticipation. They crossed a stormy Atlantic and from New York took the first train south.

Somehow neither Carie nor Andrew could stay the year out. Carie, returning to the big white house, missed intolerably the little old arrogant white-haired figure of her father. His room, which had been such a treasure shop of hand-wrought jewelry and precious stones in strange settings, of watches and clocks of every kind, was now empty and Cornelius's son lived in it. Carie did not belong to the big house any more. She was a guest only now, an infrequent guest, who returned after long periods of exile. Cornelius's wife possessed the place calmly and it was as though all the old life were gone, even to the very memory that it ever was.

In the village Andrew's brother had died and a stranger stood in the pulpit of the white church. Neale Carter was dead too, and his place had been sold to summer visitors. Almost all the old faces were gone. The very name of the town had been changed. It was strange and sad to her and she could not stay in it.

But there were Edwin and his small family and there was Comfort to see settled into school, and she turned to these and for six months lived in Edwin's house. The baby was a delight to her, whose bosom was ever a resting place for babies and whose heart was rich enough in maternity for all the babies in the world. But still, here too, in this young house, she was only a guest.

There was no home for her in her own country any more, no place where she belonged. She saw Comfort in college and saw her become absorbed in the new life and companionships, and it came to Carie then with sadness that in this country of hers no one really needed her, not even her own children whose lives were taken up now in activities in which she had no share. Then she must go back again across the sea, for there were those who did need her, who marked her absence sorely and with eagerness waited for her return. Never once when she had come back to America did she decide the question of her return to China, for each time it seemed to her that surely this time she could not bear to leave her own country again. But now she turned her face toward the exile and steadily she turned, for all of America now, her America, was in her heart and in her memories.

I think some premonition in her sensitive soul told her that this was the last time she would ever again cross the sea. Whether it was that she was even now sickening with the seed of the tropical disease which left her permanently weakened and so hastened her death, or whether she felt her country indifferent to her so that there was no home there for her, I do not know. But she was in her heart bidding farewell to all the beauty of America.

Through the long bright autumn she spent in her son's

home she walked much in the woods alone, gazing her fill of ruddy and golden trees and drinking in the last long vision of mists lying purple over the hills. She watched with affection the homes, the quiet, cleanly, contented people, the little churches filled decorously of a Sunday with families, fathers and mothers and children. Best of all in America to her were the people, the fortunate happy people who may all their lives live in America. It seemed to her sometimes that she must make them see how happy was their lot, to live in a land such as was not elsewhere in the world. But she could not speak easily of deep things. She could only smile a little and painfully when people wondered and asked her if she really wanted to "go back to that heathen country." I think to the very end of her life she was homesick for the America she had known.

What this year meant to her I scarcely knew myself until one morning when I stood beside her in church as a hymn was being sung, that one which begins "Oh beautiful for spacious skies." Her voice had been ringing out joyously but suddenly she was silent and I looked at her to see what was wrong. Her face was broken with weeping and I heard her whispering over and over, "Oh, America—America!"

She went back, therefore, and this time there was only Faith to take with them. She crossed the Pacific Ocean, ill as ever, but with the quiet conviction that it was for the last time.

In Shanghai there was again Wang Amah's faithful brown face, wrinkled and toothless now under her scanty white hair. The old servant and friend had ceased to do much of the work but she lived on with Carie for several years more until later she went to her adopted son's home because she needed constant care and she would not have Carie burdened. But now Carie took the hard old brown hand in hers and together they all went back to the bungalow. Before her, she told herself, were the long peaceful years of her age and she could look at them and be steadfast.

But Carie's life was not built for peace. The very times conspired against her and the catastrophe of the Chinese revolution burst upon the country and swept them all into its confusion. For eleven years there had been a strange, stunned quiet over China—unwonted quiet, unwonted safety for all.

Suddenly events began to occur with a rapidity which showed that peace had been only on the surface and underneath vast upheavals were taking place. The Manchu dynasty in Peking was overthrown and the arch revolutionist, Sun Yat-sen, declared China a republic.

Carie had been in her house scarcely a few months before the American consul advised all Americans to withdraw to the coast lest in the general stir and lack of central control lawless persons attack white people. Carie and Andrew looked at each other. Must they pass through the old troubles again? Andrew said half-heartedly, "You had better go," and half-heartedly, Carie packed a few things together. On the morning when all were to leave together Carie felt unwell—I doubt whether as unwell as she thought she was—and declared she could not go. They were left behind and the next day Carie recovered and triumphantly unpacked and settled herself to see the revolution through. She no longer had little children at her skirts and moreover she hated above all things the appearance of running from danger.

The heaviest fighting took place in Nanking, some miles up the river, but in her bed Carie could hear the deep reverberation of modern cannon the Chinese had learned from the West to use. Once she heard the sharp crack of rifles very near the house and with the usual recklessness dashed to a window to see what it was.

There, hiding in the bamboos outside the compound wall, she saw crouching figures. She hurried into her clothes and swiftly she went downstairs, saying nothing to anyone. Outside she found these refugees were women, Manchu women, beautifully dressed in long silk gowns, their hair dressed high and their feet unbound after the fashion of Manchu women. Some of them wore Chinese garments as a disguise, but their high cheekbones and big feet betrayed them. It came to her in a flash that they were the wives and daughters of the Manchu officials in the city, now at the mercy of a dynastic change. It was ever the custom in China that when a dynasty fell the incoming rulers killed off all surviving members of the old ruling class, and these poor creatures suffered the same fate. Carie beckoned to one tentatively to come into her house to hide, but the women shrank away into the long grass terrified, and wringing her hands in impotence, the one thing she could not bear, Carie went back. True it was that she could do no good; she might even bring more harm down on them if as a foreigner she tried to help.

On that day none can tell how many Manchu women and children and men were wantonly massacred there and all over China. Carie sat in her room with Faith and they shut their eyes and tried not to hear the sounds around them. I think the cruelty of that day was too much for Carie, accustomed as she was to sad sights, and she could never forget the pity of those ladies, delicately nurtured and sheltered all their lives, hunted now like deer and lying among the bamboos dead, their satin gowns spotted with blood.

But when those days were passed and the Chinese republic was established in form at least, Carie took great interest in the change. She was a born rebel, and rebellion always interested her. Her own country was a republic, and because of that she felt that the republican form of government was best. She turned hopefully to the new future.

"Maybe they will clean things up a little now," she used to say, and she approved heartily of the mandate which went forth at once that all queues were to be cut off from the heads of men, since the queue had been a sign of servitude exacted by the foreign Manchu dynasty. To be sure, she found considerable humor sometimes in the practical carrying out of the mandate and had as well sympathy for the staid and conservative old Chinese who considered his queue an essential part of his person. Farmers coming innocently into the city gates in the morning, their baskets of fresh vegetables slung on a pole across their shoulders, found themselves caught and seized and their hair hacked off with a pair of rude shears wielded by a soldier stationed at the gate. More than one broke into a howl of terror, thinking his life was being cut away from him with his hair.

But temporarily the new government was vigorous, and everywhere soldiers were stationed to snip off the old sign of subserviency, and many a man in those days went out in the morning with the pride of his hair and came crawling home at nightfall like a shamed dog, his hair chopped off at his nape. But to Carie it was in the end a good thing. She insisted that her gardener and man-servant cut their hair also and she viewed the shorn heads as a step toward her code of cleanliness and righteousness.

The city was left in peace again after a short time and the revolution moved northward and there was no immediate change after all greater or more fundamental than the cutting off of queues. Carie, after the excitement had swept on, found herself faced by life much as it had been, and now she set herself wholly to the missionary work in the way she had planned as soon as the children could leave her free. Faith was old enough to be sent away to school in Shanghai, and this left no child in the home, and Carie's hands were half idle.

Now she went everywhere with Andrew on his long journeys by junk and wheelbarrow and sedan chair. During these recent years a railway had been put through to the coast and she used this also as a main line of travel, branching out from it for many miles north and south and going into market towns and cities and villages, and walking miles along the countryside. Where Andrew preached she gathered about her groups of women and children and taught them to read and to sing and to knit and do handwork, and in the teaching tried to impart as well the simple essentials of Christian living and conduct.

But all this she did in her own way and never as Andrew did it. He gave his message as one who comes a stranger to a strange land, bearing a letter from the king of his own country. It was his duty to read the message that all might hear it. That duty done, his responsibility ended.

I think it was at this time that Carie realized that she and Andrew, although they had been husband and wife for more than thirty years and had had seven children together, were yet very far apart. She had married a man for the stern puritan side of her, but as life had carried her on it was the rich human side of her that had deepened and grown. Alone together in the house, alone on the junks, alone plodding side by side through the dusty country roads or along the crowded cobbled streets of cities, there was no talk to be made between them. Carie, whose cheerful, humorous, running conversation was a delight to so many others, found that to Andrew her racy comments on what she saw were often only a weariness and unwarranted audacities. His somewhat pedantic speech, his slow rare humor, his complete absorption in his task, his inability to face or to understand the practical difficulties in human lives, his own ascetic and rigorous life which held no place for beauty or pleasure, came to repel her, even while she admired his self-control and his exaltation of spirit.

She had had visions once of working with him side by side in a comradeship full and invincible. While her children were small and her life full of duties she had been able to achieve little of this comradeship, but now that the children were grown, she could, she thought, go with him into everything. They would read together, she planned, talk together, work together, and he would teach her how to improve herself and how to deepen her spiritual life, and he could explain to her the things she did not understand in the Scriptures. And she—surely there were ways she could help him, complement him. She could help with the music now more than ever in church; she could help him to choose the really lovely hymns instead of the usual grave ones that nobody liked very well, and with her gift for clever and forceful expression could lighten a little, perhaps, his somewhat dry preaching. They could go over his sermons together before he delivered them and she could suggest stories, examples, interesting analogies.

She plunged with all her old gay vigor into this new period of her life, joyously, never questioning whether Andrew wanted her help or not. It seemed to her that these were the years for which she had really left her own country; these were the years which were to make that sacrifice worth while. She said to herself that surely Andrew would gladly use her strength, as she could use his, each supplementing the other.

But she was wrong. Andrew preferred not to have his sermons aided in any way. He was quite satisfied with them and extremely doubtful that she added anything to them by her suggestions, and as for the hymns she liked, he thought them strange and meaningless and too lively for religious decency. It was not meet to sing of gladness and of the beauty of this world when beyond it hell yawned.

He was imbued, moreover, with the Pauline doctrine of the subjection of the woman to the man and to him it was enough if she kept his house and bore his children and waited on his needs. "The man is head of the woman." Through man only could she approach God. So the Scriptures taught. True, it was well if Carie taught some of the women in the churches as far as she was able, but he must have the final examination in the faith and knowledge of all and his must be the final decision, as priest of God, whether or not they were to come into the congregation.

When Carie perceived his mind, all her swift, rebel blood boiled. It seemed to her that for the first time she saw this saint of hers that she had married for his goodness, as he really was—for all his goodness toward her he was narrow and selfish and arrogant. What—was she not to go to God direct because she was born a woman? Was not her brain swifter, keener, clearer than the brains of most men? Why—was God like that, Andrew's God? It was as though she had come bearing in her two hands her rich gifts of brain and body, giving them freely and as touchingly sure of appreciation as a child—and her first real and acknowledged contact with Andrew's mind.

I cannot here do otherwise than withdraw in delicacy from the spectacle of this woman, mortally wounded in her spirit. After all, I knew her too well, I was too intimately bound to her, to probe with the fingers of analysis into this part of her life which she never by conscious word revealed to any human being. True, we knew it, and sometimes in spite of herself sad and wild words broke from her. But such words never escaped unchecked, and she always grieved for them afterwards.

She had from her birth been trained in an age stern to women, stern perhaps to all who chose to follow religion. For her there was no departure from the path of marriage. However two might strain from each other, however barren might be the husks of union between them, however far they dwelt in spirit from each other, the outward bond was not to be broken. Stronger than any bond of love could ever be were the bonds of religion and duty.

Well indeed did Carie know this. She subdued herself, subdued once more the old warm, pleasure-loving nature, though at what inner cost we can never know. She began again with unwonted silence and gentleness to put her life into a quiet coming and going among humble Chinese women. There were no more large visions of building up a strong and vigorous band of women in the churches. No, she would not trouble Andrew's churches. She would only go here and there and do what she could for this one and that, whether in churches or not.

Only recently I heard a Chinese professor in a college say of her at this time, "I remember her as none other because she washed clothes even that she might save the money and have it to give to the needy. This woman was such a one as I had not seen before or since."

Meanwhile she shrank into herself in those days and lived alone in spirit as she never had before in her days of busy motherhood. She sang to herself—softly if Andrew were in the house—and planted her garden so that it was a spot of delight to all who came to it, and these were many. She plodded back and forth by foot over the rough country roads to little thatched houses where she might meet small waiting groups of women and girls. She renewed her interest in her neighbors and servants, and sent little gifts to Wang Amah, now too old for any labor and living with her adopted son. She wrote long and loving letters to her children, and planned such little gifts as she could afford for them, and looked forward to their return to her if they would come.

But it was after all a makeshift life. Something dimmed her. She was one who needed to do great tasks, for she could do them. All the lovely, rich out-pouring of her nature seemed somehow pent up. She was perhaps one of the loneliest creatures in the world at this time of her life, for she had to have intimate love. While her children were little they had given it to her so that she scarcely missed it elsewhere. Now that they were grown and out of the home her life seemed intolerably empty.

"It would be so nice," she used to murmur sometimes, "to have someone to take a little walk with—someone of one's own."

This she said watching Andrew's figure going alone down the winding road. It would not occur to him, wrapped in his thoughts and services as he was always, to ask her to go with him, and she was too proud to suggest it. Strange remote soul of a man that could pierce into the very heavens and discern God with such certainty and never see the proud and lonely creature at his side! To him she was only a woman. Since those days when I saw all her nature dimmed I have hated Saint

Paul with all my heart and so must all true women hate him, I think, because of what he has done in the past to women like Carie, proud free-born women, yet damned by their very womanhood. I rejoice for her sake that his power is gone in these new days.

She aged very much during these years. She grew small and thin, pitifully thin, although her carriage was as erect and gallant as ever. Her heavy long hair was white as snow without a dark thread in it, and sprang softly alive from her forehead. This hair of hers brought out a certain likeness in her to Hermanus, her father, and although she no longer, had so much of his fire and militancy, yet at any time this vitality would break out for a little while in laughter and speech or quick appreciation of a joke.

She read her Bible somewhat wistfully these days, although she very seldom mentioned God. I think she was fumbling a little in the old search for Him because now she felt herself growing old and she had not done any of the things she had planned. And all these years in spite of all God had not really made a sign to her—not really so that she could not mistake it for something accidental. She used to cut out little verses and poems from papers and magazines and slip them between the pages of her Bible. The pages were stuffed with clippings, simple, sad little verses most of them, or bits of description of nature she had liked. After she was dead I read them all and reading knew her thought at this time. They were poems about little dead children, about exiles far from home, and over and over again about the God who must be taken on faith because none has ever seen Him.

In her sixtieth year she yielded suddenly to the tropical disease that had been for long, it was afterwards found, eating its way into her life. It was a disease of which neither cause nor cure is known, except that it can sometimes be cured by certain diets. It is rare to the natives of the tropics but common to white people living there.

Carie's fine constitution had been worn down by malaria and dysentery, often repeated, and so this disease wrought its havoc more rapidly on her, and although she was at first most unwilling to go to bed it became evident that a struggle for her life was ahead of her. Comfort came back to her at once, now a grown young woman and graduated from college. Into the care of her mother Comfort threw herself ardently.

Once Carie went to bed she grew worse. For a few exhausted days of almost constant sleep—for she had not taken to her bed until she literally could walk no more—she lay silent. Then after these days were over she suddenly rallied with a great effort of will, making up her mind that a task was ahead of her to which she must summon all her power if she would live. Nothing was of greater challenge to Carie than such a task. She grew suddenly immensely cheerful.

"I have decided not to die," she announced gaily one morning. "I am not going to be beaten by this old body of mine—I am young yet! I have thought of a lot of things I want to do—nice pleasant things. I have been foolish. I haven't been enjoying life enough for a long time. I am going to enjoy myself from now on."

She took herself in hand as though she were her own physician. The doctor was astounded at the change in her. She entered with immense zest in her own cure, discussing with him every possible detail as detachedly as though it were any other than herself of whom they spoke. Her disease was one of which doctors knew little. Therefore, she had Comfort write to everyone of whom she had ever heard who had recovered from it.

"No use asking about the dead ones," she remarked in high good humor.

When the letters came back it was evident that cure depended upon diet. The puzzling thing was that the diet seemed to differ with each person. It was apparently a disease of some idiosyncratic deficiency.

"I'll have to find out at last what my personal peculiarity is," she laughed. "I have always feared I had one!"

Milk seemed helpful to many. She went on a diet of milk alone for two months, sipping small quantities every two hours. It was no use. Her flesh fell away until she was dreadful to see. Only her dark eyes looked bright and indomitable out of her little shrunken face.

"I'll be like Alice in Wonderland soon," she remarked one morning when Comfort was helping her bathe. She looked at her withered limbs. "I'll have to nibble something else to make me bigger before I melt away altogether."

She tried buttermilk then, made with rennet tablets. That was a little better, for at least she did not lose for a month. But by now June had come and with it the summer heat, humid and heavy with moisture from the flooded rice fields.

We took her then to Kuling to the little stone cottage, a difficult journey with her poor bones so bare that a thick padded mattress had to be put under them before she could be touched.

But the air of the mountain tops helped her at once and suddenly she heard of a new remedy. Someone had recovered on liver soup and spinach juice. She began to take the nauseous mixture with immense enthusiasm. Her couch stood out on the little veranda, and she lay there sipping her soup and gazing out over the tree tops into the valley below. We knew she was thinking of the beauty and voluntarily using it to take her mind from what she had to drink.

How we watched the scales that first week! She gained two ounces. By the end of the first month she had gained a pound and a half. Certain symptoms had abated, among them a sore mouth which left no least part of the mucous lining healthy. She was greatly encouraged and very cheerful with such a piece of work to do.

She did a great deal of thinking these days, of which we caught glimpses in fragments of speech about it.

"You know, I am going to be immensely selfish when I get well. I am really going to take care of myself!" When we laughed ironically at this a glint of humor lit her eyes with mischief. "Yes, I am going to get my hands really nice!"

Then she painted for us in words the picture of the dear, delightful old lady she was going to be, sweet, dignified, immaculately dressed. When we laughed again at this, knowing full well that the moment she had strength enough to walk she would be running about among her poor again and grubbing between times in her garden's black earth, she said somewhat seriously for her, "No, I mean it. I've been silly to be sad. I am going to love life more than ever. All my life I've been doing things for others and now I am going to be so selfish you won't know me. I've always wanted secretly to have time to be selfish! I am going to read as many books and magazines as I like. I am going to have a new lavender silk dress. I am going to make little visits to my friends. Do you know, in spite of the hundreds of visitors in our house I've never been away on just a pleasure visit to anyone? I always had to go and do something for someone."

But convalescence in that disease is not steady. The summer passed for Carie in a series of progresses and relapses, but the measure of her real progress was the seriousness of each relaspe, and for her each relapse was less than the previous one. She was winning the battle.

Autumn approached and the time came when we must go back to our fields of work, but Carie decided she would stay on alone in the mountains and finish her fight. She longed for Wang Amah who was too old and feeble to come, so with the manservant she had Carie stayed on alone in the cottage and set herself to her work on her own body.

I have had to piece from her letters the story of Carie's life that autumn and winter. She gained slowly but steadily, lying out on the veranda watching the leaves turn and drop away. A deep russet glow lay over the whole hillside and purple asters bloomed. It was the nearest she had ever come to the autumn in her own country and she felt the peace of beauty soak into her recovering body.

The day came when she could rise and walk a little, and every day she massaged her own limbs and took sunbaths and kept to her careful diet, enlarging it bit by bit to include more and more foods. Sometimes she made a mistake and took something that gave her a setback, but she viewed herself as one quite detached and sent us reports on herself as though she were her own patient. Gradually from some experimenting she worked out a diet suited to her and she began to improve more rapidly and before many days was creeping down the steps and into the little ferny garden and then soon she walked a little along the pebbly mountain road that ran just above the house.

Then it seemed only a short time until she was visiting others less well than herself, a few invalids who were in the valley to regain health, and then instead of herself the letters were about them. She visited each regularly and soon had their life stories and the detailed accounts of their illnesses, giving in return, I am sure, vast amounts of practical advice. She became absorbed in one middle-aged American woman who had the same disease as her own, and she studied the case, as freshly eager to help as any youth. She had the satisfaction of seeing the woman recover.

As winter came on Carie's health returned fast and she was restless and eager to be doing something. She recovered her buoyancy and awareness of all around her. But enough of the symptoms of the disease remained so that her doctor would not let her leave the mountain air. She conceived the idea, then, of using the time to rebuild the cottage.

The cottage had grown frail with age and the woodwork was rotten with white ants and the rubble stone was loosened in many places. Moreover, with Comfort home again and with Faith to come, the cottage was too small.

Nothing could be more joy to her than replanning the little house, although it must be at a minimum of expenditure. Still, it would be fun to look over all the old material and see what could be used again. It would be fun to make over something—fun to surprise the family! She entered into it with all her old zest and lost interest in her illness.

She called a Chinese contractor and bit by bit went over the whole cottage with him testing the wood and trying the stone to see what was usable. Finally they decided all the stone was good except for a little shale that had crumbled and the big beams could all be used again. She drew a plan that had three tiny bedrooms, two small baths, a big porch and a living room with a big stone fireplace. Underneath where the hill sloped to allow it there would be two service rooms. With the closest care, remembering Father's New Testament, all this could be done for an amazingly small amount of money.

She moved into an empty house nearby, and with the greatest enthusiasm watched the old house razed and the new foundations set. From morning to night she pottered about the place, judging the placing of the stone and exulting over the rising walls. She made it American from roof to basement as far as she could. She hunted in the streams with a coolie for the smooth stones that were to make the wide fireplace. In one of the bedrooms she had a little fireplace put. I think she half dreamed that some day in her old age she might come here to live and thus seem almost in America. At heart, although she would not acknowledge it, she had already said farewell to America from which the cruel sea separated her— America, also, who does not receive back with eagerness those of her children who leave her, even though they love her.

This was a happy winter for Carie. She was happy because she was making something, and she felt the return of health to her mind and her body. She was, besides, living in the midst of the loveliest nature, and away from poor and oppressed people. I remember her writing of one of the ice storms they had on the mountains that winter, when every twig and every leaf of bamboo and vine were encrusted with ice, and when the sun came out, "It is too beautiful even for me, who can eat and drink beauty for my daily bread and not be surfeited," she wrote us.

She did all sorts of gay things that winter. There was a little school for American children at the time and she delighted to go tobogganing with the children. I have a little snapshot of her sitting at the head of the sledful of children, the guiding ropes in her hands, her eyes dark and bright, and her face full of laughter. She did the things she had not done since she was a girl, and there was no one to be displeased with her merriment.

When we all went back in August for our month's vacations, she received us in the new cottage, prouder than if it had been a palace. She had worked hard to have it ready, even to the white muslin curtains in the windows and fresh mats on the floors and green ferns in hanging baskets and flowers everywhere. It was the home of her heart, her picture of America that she had borne ever in her heart and made actual in this transplanted spot. How she loved it!

And, indeed, it was a lovesome place, the little, clean stone house set in a small terraced lawn among the tree tops that grew on the slope of the hill. Through the trees one caught glimpses of the opposite mountain and through the gap in the further hills there was the blue vista of the distant plains. Inside, the cottage was as simple as poverty itself but how fresh and clean and how swept with mountain winds and mists! I believe she could bear sometimes to think that she might never see America again.

But after the summer she grew sober one day and said she had played long enough and must go back to work. Andrew needed his home and she knew what the house must be like with her not there. Moreover, during the summer Comfort had become engaged to be married to a young American, and there was that to be thought of, a wedding in a few months. Faith had finished high school in Shanghai and must be prepared for the return to America to college. There were these tasks ahead and she faced them eagerly.

All during the winter we watched her, and she maintained a steady if not a robust health, indeed, a well-being that was astonishing for one who had lain so emaciated. She kept to her diet and unwillingly she rested. Meanwhile she planned the wedding and planned for Faith and was happy and busy once more—synonymous words with her.

Spring came and the wedding was quite as perfect as she had planned it to be. It might have been on the lawn of any American home, a simple affair at sunset with a few friends gathered and Comfort a tall and slender young bride walking casually in her white gown and bride's veil to meet her groom. Carie watched with a thrill of new life stirring. These two of hers, the new life to come to her from them, the new interests—how foolish for her to think there had been nothing left for her to do!

She looked unusually lovely herself that day, with her snowy hair piled high, curly and abundant, and her dark and vivid eyes young as ever. She wore a silvery grey dress and carried a great armful of pale pink carnations. The wedding cake she made and iced herself and it stood under the wistaria arbor and she watched the young bride cut it, and when all was over we heard her murmur in great content, "It really couldn't have been a lovelier wedding in America."

Eight years had passed since Andrew had been in America and now the time had come when he was free to go once more on a furlough. Carie was torn between her great longing to see America once more and the frailness of her body which the doctor said would not stand the racking of another sea journey. I do not know when she made the final renunciation. Perhaps she did not make it all in one moment; she was very silent about it, and we did not know until almost the end whether she would go or not. She decided that she would not go, that Andrew must take Faith home and then come back in the half year. She would stay on alone in the house and keep his work together for him as best she could until he came back.

As if to confirm her in her decision the word came of the death of Cornelius, and to think of his beloved face gone, this brother who was more than brother to her youth, made her give up more easily the last thought of going home. No, she would keep America now where it would always be most alive for her, in her heart and memory. Too many faces were gone, too many new things had come, and there would be no place for her at all, perhaps. Even Edwin seemed very far away, absorbed in his work and in his own children, not needing her any more.

She wrote him still her long weekly letters, tender toward him as though he were still the small son of her youth, as indeed he was to her. Andrew would never think to see what the babies looked like, but she adjured Faith to write all the details of hair and eyes and cunning ways. She longed for these grandchildren of hers inexpressibly, yet she was comforted, for they were in America, safe, as everyone was safe there.

Thus she was left quite alone in the old square mission house, the house in which she had been accustomed to hear the voices of her children, where Andrew had prayed and studied and from which he had gone forth on his long journeys; where there had been much coming and going of others, now she was quite alone.

I never once heard her say she was afraid. The old manservant she kept to help her in her garden slept downstairs in the servants' quarters and except for him there was no other. She bought herself at some odd shop an old and rusty pistol which she had not the faintest idea how to fire, but two or three times during the night she would rise and promenade through the house with it in one hand, a candle in the other.

During the unsettled years after the first revolution there was danger in her being alone like this, but her neighbors knew her well, and she was never afraid. She used to say she had no time to be afraid because she was always first angry at anyone's daring to try to make her so. I remember that once in earlier years during a hot summer's night she heard a noise at the open window of the sleeping room. She leaped to her feet and drew aside a screen placed at the foot of her bed. There in the window stood a tall Chinese who stared at her wickedly.

"Get down out of there!" she called to him in her vehement, ready fashion. "What are you doing here in my house?"

She ran to him, a small, white-robed figure in her old-fashioned nightgown, and he wavered and fell backward to disappear among the shadows of the garden, strewing the towels and pillow cases he had stolen.

Andrew, who had a curious, nervous fear of thieves, remained in bed, much to Carie's indignation, who after urging him vainly to get up, dashed out barefoot to pursue the thief. She called to servants as she ran but they dressed with careful slowness, being terrified of thieves in a country where every thief carried a knife. But Carie rushed out into the dewy moonlit lawn, oblivious to centipedes and scorpions, and reached the compound wall in time to snatch at a bag she saw disappearing over it and to hang on to it with all her strength, still continuing her scream of abusive Chinese. She was rewarded by having someone drop the other end of the bag. Carie collected the various things scattered about the garden, and by this time Andrew was up, somewhat sheepish as even saints may be, and the servants, now that the thieves were gone, were all in a bustle. Carie retrieved thus most of her slender stock of linen and went back to bed in great triumph.

"You might have been killed. It was very foolish," said Andrew reproachfully.

It was the first time Carie had thought of that possibility. She replied thoughtfully, "I suppose it was. But I was just so mad to think someone would come into my house like that. Besides, what are you going to do—let a rascal walk off with your things and never say a word?"

No, I don't believe she was ever afraid in her life. Indeed, she had the greatest scorn of physical cowardice, and this was a further wedge between Andrew and herself, Andrew, who could face any danger in the pursuit of his duty, but apart from duty could be timorous. Carie could never understand this timorousness, born of a nature shy and diffident, who dwelled apart from reality.

But she did not, although she was alone, shut herself up in loneliness. She went every day among the people far and near and came home at night desperately weary but with her face content and quiet. I asked her often what she did, but she was always a little vague. "Oh, nothing much," she used to reply cheerfully.

It seemed to be the same old human work she had always done, coming and going among people. I don't think she preached much beyond saying that we must all try to believe in God and try to do what He liked us to do. Certainly He would like people to take better care of their little children, and men not to be hard on their wives, and wives to keep nice homes for their husbands and children, and to keep things as clean as they could. She taught young girls to read, I know, young girls who hungered for a little learning denied them by their social system. She used to talk about many things in the world, describing other countries she had seen. I have seen her talking like this to a group of women, plain creatures who had little in their lives besides the bearing of children and the round of dingy house cares, and they listened to her, their mouths open and their eyes dreaming. She told them about the stars and the planets and she told them of the sea and its strange life and made them feel they were part of a great and wonderful universe. I have never seen her other than most tender to those of her own sex who had no hope from the very misfortune of their birth.

But she could be very angry at the mother of a little, weeping, footbound girl, and now and again she prevailed by her sheer persistence. Now and again, too, she threw herself into the rescue of some opium addict. I know one poor old sot whom she rescued quite against his will by weeks of vigilance. That she prevailed at last and that he was delighted to find himself free from the burden that had kept him and his family in debt he ascribed to her prayers and to her religion, and who am I to say he was wrong, since for him, as for many others, the new religion of Christ was typified in Carie and in her passionate interest in his recovery.

"It must be so, for no one else would have cared enough what I was or if my family starved or not," he concluded simply.

I believe Carie enjoyed the struggle as she always did any task that looked insuperable, and certainly she made the old man's life miserable for him at times, but still the upshot of it was that he was cured and went back to being a weaver and to supporting his family.

She had around her at this time a whole circle of old women who craved friendship and interest in their small affairs, and who had outlived any such interest on the part of their families to whom they were only burdens. They knew too well Carie's softness of heart and that even after her angers were over she would slip them some money or a basket of food or a bit of cloth for a coat.

There was, too, her Chinese daughter, now the mother of six children, in each of whom Carie felt she had a share, and besides these many others whom she visited and who visited her and with whom she held long and intimate conversations on their affairs. I dare say if this American woman had set herself to the writing of novels she could have produced a score of books filled with the tales of lives she knew as no other white person I have ever seen has known them.

If she hated the faults and sins of people she was generous and quick to see their virtues, too, and she never failed to enjoy a joke even though it turned against herself. Once she bought a rug to put before her organ, a little gay rug bought at some sacrifice, because it pleased her. One day a chance acquaintance of Andrew's came in to talk over, as he said, the "new religion." Andrew talked with the man for a while and as he rose to leave, told him that he would walk with him a little way and talk further if the man would wait until he changed into other shoes, for it was winter and the roads were bad. Carie was upstairs and when Andrew came up she decided she would walk also, and the three of them started out. The Chinese went a little way, spoke of an appointment and turned down a side street. When Carie and Andrew came home, Carie's swift eyes noticed at once something lacking in the room. It was the little new rug. While he had talked of religion the man had noted it, and when Andrew had left him alone he had folded it and stuffed it inside his capacious winter robe. Much as Carie hated to lose the rug she laughed until the tears came at the incident, remembering with fresh laughter the man's pious face and earnest voice and the rug in his bosom. She could not but laugh at his cleverness while she hated it and she upset Andrew very much by remarking, "I hope he isn't your typical inquirer, Andy, or we'll have to give up housekeeping!"

She was tolerant always, however, where no evil was meant. I remember once another American's saying with some impatience, "I resent very much this name of 'foreign devil' which the people shout at us so much. Surely they must know we do them good sometimes."

Carie smiled gently, and she answered, "Sometimes they don't know any other name for us. I remember once an old sick woman coming to me for help and she bowed and knocked her head on the ground before me and said as humbly as though she were addressing a queen, 'Please, most honorable Foreign Devil, I crave your help.' No, it depends on how they say it," she concluded.

Andrew came back at the end of eight months, somewhat dazed by a new America. These were the years just after the Great War, and he had seen a country unlike anything he had known before. That which he had held as sure as heaven itself almost, his own country, he now beheld shaken and bewildered and cynical of the very things for which his fathers had fought and established themselves upon its new shores. He was not one who was able to relate at any great length his own experiences, but bit by bit Carie extracted from him parts of a picture which her keen mind was able to fit together, a picture of a country awry and beside itself—and it was her own country!

She began to regret deeply at this time that she was old and helpless and could do nothing for her own land. She said many times to us, "I wish I had my life now to live over again, young and new. Do you know what I would do? I would go to New York and to those places where foreigners come into our gates and I would spend my life telling them what America means and what they must do and be to make America. I think that is why America is not herself now—too many people do not understand what it is to be an American."

Again and again she said, "I wish I had my life to live over again. I would live it for America. I am glad my son is there. He will do something for me for America."

I think during these next two years she was constantly troubled by this desire. She read everything she could find about modern America, trying to fathom if she could the causes for America's plight. Where once in that fair and peaceful land she had heard the call of others less fortunate, now again she seemed to hear a call, this time the cry of her own in need. In the impotence of her age and situation she grieved a good deal and prayed more for her country than she had prayed for anything in a long time.

She did not perceive that her body was growing thinner and thinner and that symptoms of extreme anemia were upon her. The old disease had left her inwardly impaired and without knowing it she had been eating less and less, and if she gave a thought to her increasing thinness it was only to suppose it was because she was able to eat so little.

But one day her strength gave out suddenly and she could not even walk up the stairs to her room. Comfort came hastily, her eyes sharp with love, and she saw at once that this was something serious. She settled herself to stay until Carie was well again, and in spite of her mother's vigorous objections—Carie seemed never too ill to object vigorously to what she did not want—Comfort called a doctor.

Things were bad indeed. An insidious heart weakness made a needed operation impossible, and from the very first there was little hope. Carie, reading quickly as she always did the faces of others, saw what Comfort would have hidden and some of her old stubbornness came to her aid.

"I am not going to die," she maintained in spite of her feebleness. "I haven't had time to do a lot of the things I had planned. There are a lot of books I want to read yet and there are many people who need me. Besides—" she added with a twinkle, "I haven't got my hands nice yet. No, no—I am going to have ten good years more when I shall really settle down to being a nice old lady and wear pretty lavender dresses and be a grandmother to my children's children." And then as though the realization of her weakness came over her, she cried out in a sort of anger against God, "Anyway, I won't die until Faith comes home and I see her again."

It was the long fight for life once more.

Once again we carried her on coolies' backs up the mountains to the stone cottage, a bone-thin, indomitable creature, her young and changeless dark eyes looking bravely out of the small face under the mass of white hair.

Once more she set herself bravely to the curing of her body. It was a good body, sound in heritage, but it had been made to respond too often to rally now to her will. It became evident that it would not rally again. She knew it well, and there was a short period, a matter of a few days, when we beheld the spectacle of a young and brave spirit viewing with anger and dismay the old and feeble body which must die. She spoke no word to anyone beyond the courteous words of necessity, but the look of her eyes was terrible, and we turned away in agony at what we saw there.

Then it was over. She accepted it. It was as though she gave her body up then as negligible and worth nothing to her, and she set herself to fulfil the desires of her spirit during the last months. Not that she ever spoke of death. She did not, ignoring the whole matter, and dwelling more than ever upon the beauty she loved above every other part of her life. She spoke often of the sweetness of the bird calls in the trees about the house, of the green shadows on the grass, of the splendor of the lilies on the terrace. At sunset she lay quite still and let her eyes range over the clouds and the vista of the valleys.

Whether she thought of the future or not, I do not know. She was a dauntless woman, fortified now by life to meet resolutely whatever was to come. She indulged in no dying cant of God, who even yet had made her no sign. It seemed that she realized that none, no, not one, could say for a certainty what lay ahead of the moment when she must go forth and alone.

In those last days she laid hold of life as she never had, even she, a woman greedy and zestful for life as she had ever been. At the end of the summer we took her back to the bungalow on the river and by then we all knew she must die. But she gave no sign of her own knowledge of this beyond the great quiet with which she met the nights and days. Sometimes in the deep night when the darkness pressed upon her and she grew faint and breathless, she turned her enormous eyes toward Comfort who was with her and she asked the old question her own mother had asked, "Child—is this—*death?*"

And when Comfort cried out passionately, "I will not let you die!" she smiled and said, "How like me you are —so I told my mother, too."

One day she said, "There are so many things I have not heard of or seen—so many pleasures. Not one of you knows how I love pleasure! I want a victrola. I want to hear music of all the kinds I have not heard."

We sent to the coast city for a victrola and for records and she lay listening by the hour. What she thought I do not know, only she would have no mournful music. Once someone put on the record, "O rest in the Lord, Wait patiently for Him," and she said with a quiet and profound bitterness, "Take that away. I have waited and patiently—for nothing."

We never played it again and to this day I cannot endure that music for the memory it brings back of her voice—not a sorrowful voice, but quiet, proud, resigned, courageous. She had faced by this time the truth, that the search for God with which she had begun her life was not in her time to be fulfilled.

Toward the end as she became weaker it was evident that she must have a specially trained nurse, one who knew how to lift and tend her. She had not heretofore been willing to have one about her, having a curious and profound distrust of the professional. Now the only way we could persuade her was to use the argument of weariness in caring for her night and day, and instantly she was anxious to spare us. The poison of the disease was creeping through her body now and her hearing and sight were dimmed, and she slept a great deal, although she had times of great clarity, and indeed whole days when she was herself almost completely.

I can never forget the coming of that nurse. We sent to a hospital in Shanghai, but it had been difficult to find anyone on account of an epidemic of cholera. But one was found at last in reply to our urgent telegrams and early one morning just at dawn she came to the house, and I who had been sitting through the night with Carie went to meet her on the stair.

My heart sank as I saw her, an Englishwoman of no

uncertain age, with peroxide hair and a complexion wholly synthetic. She was the very sort of person most distasteful to Carie. But in the need of the hour I let her come in and introduced her to Carie.

Carie stared out of her fading eyes fixedly at the nurse, who wore the voluminous cap of her calling as an English nurse. Then she asked with characteristic directness, "Why is that pillow case on your head?"

"I will take it off, if you like," said the nurse kindly.

"Do," replied Carie with emphasis, and when it had been done she said, "Why, what pretty hair you have, my dear, hid away like that, and so lovely with your fair skin!"

Her eyesight by this time could not see the truth of the poor creature's ruined face, and this genuine and simple praise touched the woman and won her real devotion, and from then on she nursed Carie with unfailing care.

Strange and fitting it was as an end to this generous and most human life that at the last there should come a waif out of the dregs of Shanghai to see it to the finish. To this woman Carie turned with her old interest, inquiring into her life and history with much sympathy. The woman was, I suppose, as unmoral a creature as ever lived, and one whose last remaining shreds of reserve had been swept away by the World War experience she had had, and there were many sordid places in her story which Carie passed over gently, saying only, "I know— I know how hard it is to be good—especially when no answer comes and one goes on waiting in the dark."

Then with one of her sudden changes she said, "You were speaking of dancing. Now do you know, I have always wanted to see a fox trot; I've read about them. Could you do one for me?"

This was the scene we came upon then, to the tune of a ragged bit of jazz on the victrola. Here was Carie propped up on her pillows, the image of death except for her eyes, which all dimmed as they were in sight, somehow maintained yet their old fire and flash, watching with vivid delight the white, whirling figure of the nurse. At the end of the dance when the nurse dropped breathless into a chair Carie remarked with the air of a connoisseur, "Well, that's a pretty thing—so graceful and light. I should not be surprised if Andrew is all wrong about God. I believe one ought to choose the happy, bright things of life, like dancing and laughter and beauty. I think if I had it to do over again I would choose those instead of thinking them sinful. Who knows?—God might like them."

She fell into musing a little and then into sleep. Thus did the side of her nature which she had put down so resolutely in her youth claim her again in her age and in her years of wisdom.

She turned quite against Andrew these days and would not have him beside her. Not that she bade him go, but she was obviously restless and ill at ease when she saw him, and some struggle seemed to take place in her again. Once she murmured when she saw him, "That book is still not finished after all these years—" So we kept him away, and he was bewildered but willing enough, for he had never understood her nature and the changes of which she was capable, none greater than this at the end, when she deliberately put from her all thought of religion and God and chose the beauty of life and creation in this world that she loved and knew richly.

We wheeled her bed to the window and she lay looking out contentedly. Once she said, half dreaming, "I have had after all so many of the good things of life. I have had little children at my breast, I have had good earth to garden in, ruffled curtains blowing in at my windows, hills to look at, and valleys and sky, books and my music— and people to do for. I've had a lot of good in my life. I'd like to go on living, but this time I would give my life to America."

The only deep shadow across those days was the fear of dying before Faith came back. But Faith was due any day now and she made up her mind that she would not die until Faith had come. At last the day came and at last the hour. Carie had not strength enough to allow herself to be excited, lest her heart stop with the extra burden; therefore she was very quiet and usual.

But she was determined that Faith coming back a young woman from college should not find the house sad because of the shadow of coming death. So she asked that her newest gown be put on her, a delicate lavender silk one embroidered in silver, a gift from Comfort, and she had her hair freshly done, and when all was ready, even to a bowl of rosebuds at her side, she asked—unheard of request—for a stick of chewing gum! We sent to the compradore's shop and bought it and gave it to her in great mystification, none of us ever having seen her use it before, and she lay back on her white pillows in great state, and when Faith came there she was, chewing vigorously, her eyes twinkling.

"Well, here you see your old mother!" she cried gaily, casual as though she had seen Faith but yesterday instead of three years before. "Here I am chewing gum like a fast young woman—I hear it is the thing in America these days!"

We all laughed and the tension of the moment was past. It was what she had planned, that we laugh, lest we weep. It was as if she must guard now against sorrow, lest her heart burst her frail body asunder. She accepted Faith's presence quietly and in a few days seemed to forget that she had been away.

Day after day she lay in a sleep and only occasionally now could one feel the strong spirit stoutly rousing itself once more against the approaching change. Once she lifted her two hands, swollen and sad to see. She looked at them intently and murmured to herself, "I never did get my hands nice after all. Perhaps later—"

Only once she mentioned her death. She came out of her sleep suddenly and said with great distinctness to Comfort who happened to be the one watching them,

"Child, if I should seem afraid at the end, it will be only because this old body of mine takes advantage of me for the moment. It has always been my enemy—always trying to beat me down. You just remember my spirit goes on straight. *I am not afraid!*"

Again she roused herself after that, this time to give directions regarding her tombstone. There were to be no words of commendation, no mention of wifehood or motherhood, only her own name and under that three texts, to be written in English and Chinese also, the last one that triumphant announcement, "To him that overcometh a crown of life shall be given."

Once more she roused herself to say, "Do not sing any sad hymns over me. I want the Glory Song. I hate to die. My life is unfinished. I was going to live to a hundred. But if I must die—I'll die with joy and triumph—I'll go on somehow—"

There were no last words or any sign. She died in her sleep, and at the moment of passing her face lit up with a great smile, and then fell into great gravity. But none of us knew the meaning of that smile. It was as though she simply withdrew from us all and went on alone, leaving us only her life to remember, a vivid, full, bittersweet life. We dressed her in the lavender silk gown she loved and put about her the silver grey and pale gold chrysanthemums of autumn. It was on an autumn day we buried her, a windy, misty day under a grey sky. The brave words of the song she had told us to sing over her went out like the challenge of all human life in its desperate cry against inevitable death everywhere around. Thus ended all of her life that we can know.

I suppose she would have considered her life a failure if she had judged it by the measure of what she had meant it to be. Certainly if at the beginning she could have seen the end she would have called it failure. The search for God, the need of the deep, puritanical side of her multiple spirit, was never fulfilled. I think that to one of her keen and practical mind it could not be. She was skeptical by nature, yet mystic too, lover of beauty and dreamer of the unknown.

She was one of those who, having visited the sick and those in prison and cared for the widowed and fatherless and fed the hungry and wept with those who wept and laughed with those who were merry, reproached herself that she had not chosen a better part. She was one of those who reproaching herself humbly might have said to the God she sought, "Lord, when did I all these things for You?" To such a one might He make answer, "Inasmuch—"

But if she judged her life fallen short, to us, among whom she lived, what a life it was! I do not think one of us would have called her a saintly woman. She was far too practical, far too vivid and passionate, too full of humor and change and temper for that. She was the most human person we have ever known, the most complex in her swift compassion, in her gusts of merriment and in her utter impatiences; she was best friend and companion to us.

Now that I have come to know for myself the country she loved so well, I see that indeed she was the very flower of it. Young in spirit to the end, indomitable, swift in generosity, eager after the fine things of life and yet able to live ardently if necessary in poverty, idealistic with the true idealism that is never satisfied with mere idealism not translated into actuality—she was the very breath of America made flesh and spirit.

To the thousands of Chinese whom she touched in every sort of way she was America. How often have I heard them say, "Americans are good, because they are kind. *She* was an American." To lonely sailor boys and soldier boys and to all white men and women her hearty good cheer and ready fellowship stood for home—for America in a far country. To her children, in the midst of the most remote and alien environment she gave somehow and who knows at what cost, sometimes, an American background, making them truly citizens of their own country and giving them a love of it which is deathless.

To all of us everywhere who knew her this woman was America.